A·D
ART AND DESIGN

EDITORIAL OFFICES:
42 LEINSTER GARDENS, LONDON W2 3AN
TEL: 071-402 2141 FAX: 071-723 9540

HOUSE EDITOR: Nicola Hodges
EDITORIAL TEAM: Ramona Khambatta,
Katherine MacInnes
ART EDITOR: Andrea Bettella
CHIEF DESIGNER: Mario Bettella
DESIGNER: Jason Rigby

SUBSCRIPTION OFFICES:
UK: VCH PUBLISHERS (UK) LTD
8 WELLINGTON COURT, WELLINGTON STREET
CAMBRIDGE CB1 1H7
TEL: (0223) 321111 FAX: (0223) 313321

USA AND CANADA: VCH PUBLISHERS INC
303 NW 12TH AVENUE DEERFIELD BEACH,
FLORIDA 33442-1788 USA
TEL: (305) 428-5566 / (800) 367-8249
FAX: (305) 428-8201

ALL OTHER COUNTRIES:
VCH VERLAGSGESELLSCHAFT MBH
BOSCHSTRASSE 12, POSTFACH 101161
69451 WEINHEIM
FEDERAL REPUBLIC OF GERMANY
TEL: 06201 606 148 FAX: 06201 606 184

Art & Design is published six times per year (Jan/Feb; Mar/Apr; May/Jun; Jul/Aug; Sept/Oct; and Nov/Dec). Subscription rates for 1994 (incl p&p): *Annual subscription price*: UK only £65.00, World DM 195, USA $135.00 for regular subscribers. *Student rate*: UK only £50.00, World DM 156, USA $105.00 incl postage and handling charges. *Individual issues*: £14.95/DM 39.50 (plus £2.30/DM 5 for p&p, per issue ordered), US$24.95 (incl p&p).
For the USA and Canada, *Art & Design* is distributed by VCH Publishers, Inc, 303 NW 12th Avenue, Deerfield Beach, FL 33442-1788; Telefax (305) 428-8201; Telephone (305) 428-5566 or (800) 367-8249. Application to mail at second-class postage rates is pending at Deerfield Beach, FL Postmaster: Send address changes to *Art & Design*, 303 NW 12th Avenue, Deerfield Beach, FL 33442-1788. Printed in Italy. All prices are subject to change without notice. [ISSN: 0267-3991]

CONTENTS

David Kemp, *King 'Coal'*, 1993

Chris Drury, *Whale Bundle*, Ireland, 1993

David Nash, *Red*, 1993

Some preliminary
PROPOSITIONS
towards a concept of
the new Gallery/
Museum of Modern
Art for LONDON in
the new millennium.

COMPREHENDING

the siting of an important component at

BANKSIDE

and the continuing vitality of the

MILLBANK TATE

appropriately modified to meet the requirements of

Art and the needs of the people for whom it is made.

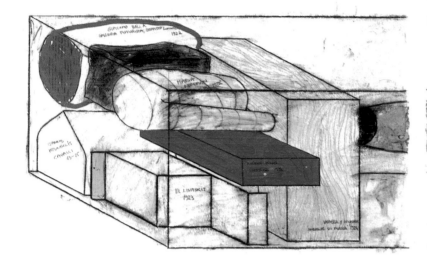

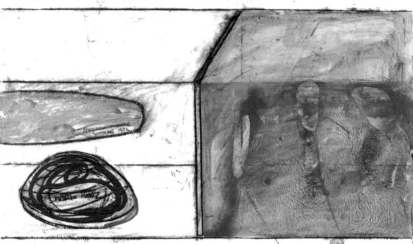

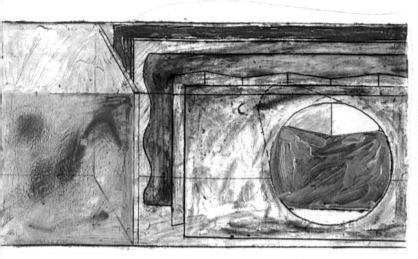

A

CONCEPTUAL TOPOGRAPHIES
(cf. Underground)

New maps for new purposes (art purposes) a new art map for London

proposition: a great conceptual dome the circumference of whose base is marked by the

Nine-Mile-Measured Museum
a continuous line of art drawn round the city centre:

the city itself conceived as a work of social sculpture; a dome of discovery

the city itself becomes an INVISIBLE museum, made visible at points of energy/contact: Nine stations of art on the perimeter line formed by

THE MONORAIL MUSEUM

THE WORLD's FIRST INF

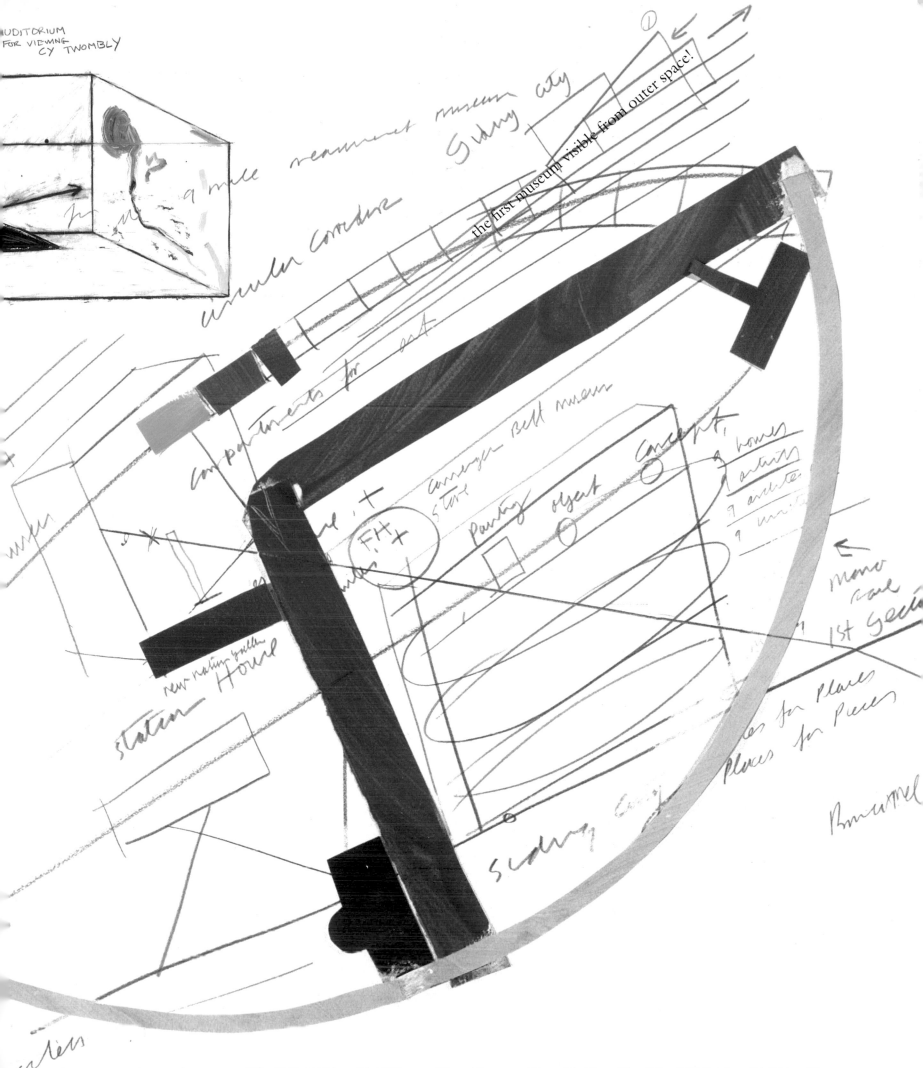

AUDITORIUM
FOR VIEWING
CY TWOMBLY

the first museum visible from outer space!

A-STRUCTURAL MUSEUM

·Sections 2–9

(7 miles: 4 stations/art works) completed to celebrate the century's turn:

the BIG WHEEL of Art

An elegant and spectacular Vasarian Corridor/walkway/ambulatory for the 21st century
(one palace of art to another; twice crossing the river)

The first section
(wedge) bisected by a line which passes
through the South Bank (The Festival Hall of 1951):
being the first sector of the new cosmology of art encompassing all arts.
At the centre a skylon/endless column/topless tower: a great aerial/
information gathering work/ Having beautiful utility: being fit for purpose in
Every station a work: continuous connection with the periphery of the circular work, and with every *a power station: the mo*
widening circle beyond across every border and boundary of the wider world.
The receiver: the Trafalgar Square Red Box THE CONCEPT MUSEUM
(concepts no objects) facing the 19th-century treasure house/store house
National Gallery (at the hub of the old empire; the centre of the new art
universe) documentation/sounds/library/art data bank:
the art mainframe for the world in
the new millennium.

ork made by artists—the axial gallery/museum

SECTION 1

consisting of a two mile circumferential section between TATE ONE and TATE TWO

TATE TO TATE

(tate–à–tate)

MILLBANK TO BANKSIDE

THE MONORAIL MUSEUM entered and exited from *within* the galleries and being c

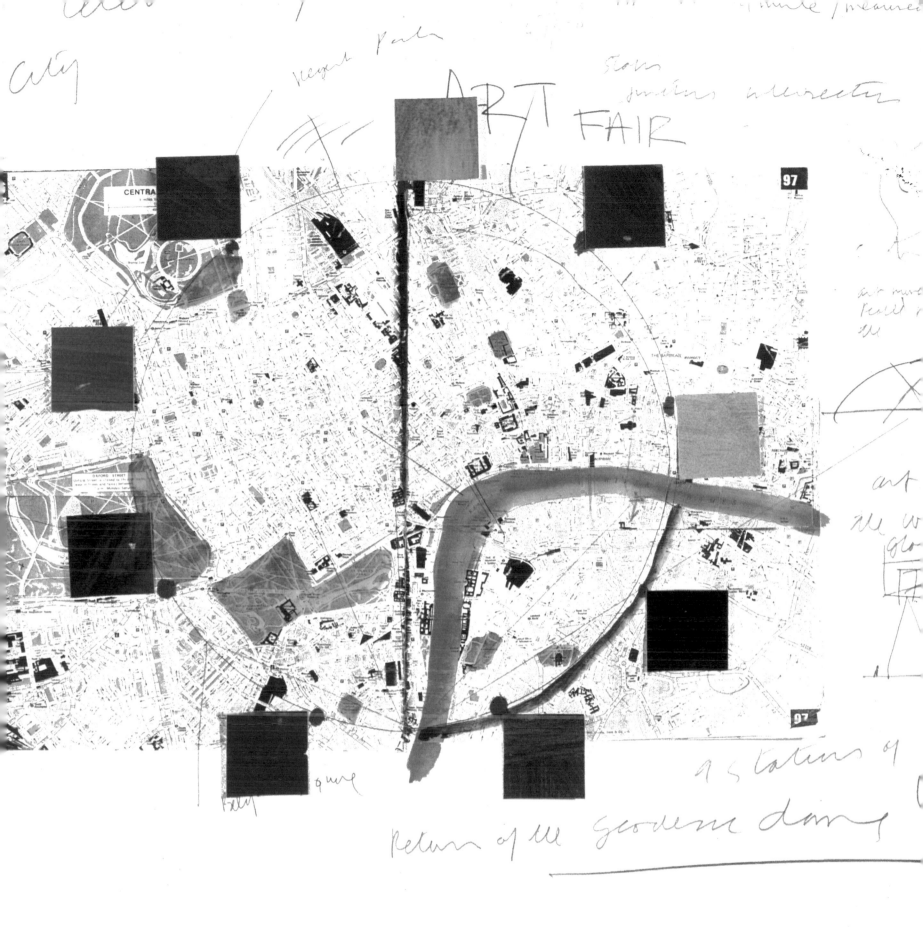

us with them: *unifying the two into one museum exemplifying the true continuities and unities of art*

B
CONCEPTUAL STRUCTURES

NB: Architectural Structures are not ruled out as works of art

NB: The box being in these propositions a conceit for a structure allowing the arrangement of infinitely flexible spaces

a concept of structure: a **paradigm** not a building

buildings will be required as the temporary realizations of structures for purposes)
(not 'form follows function' but 'function follows behaviour')

Circumstances alter showcases
(two millennia is temporary)

Powerhouse becomes powerhouse; centre of energy becomes centre of energy.

Art energy is as invisible as electricity

REQUIREMENTS FOR THE ART OF THE NEW MILLENNIUM:
Structures for modification by artists;
Structures for artists not expressive of architects;
Structures for art not expressive of architecture.

Structures that can comprehend the city or parts thereof, encompass buildings, modify given architectural facts to new facts, in accord with the architectonics of thought, feeling, creative purpose (the components of the Social Sculpture and the Conceptual Architecture of the future)

THE NEW ART PALACE may be invisible, becoming visible in time, materialize as a work

2001

'We later civilizations … We too now know that we are mortal.' Valéry

THE MOMENT when the idea of a new Museum of Modern (20c.) and
Contemporary (late 20c.) Art for LONDON is realized in prospect, its siting
agreed, its funding anticipated, is the moment precisely for a reconsideration of
its meaning and purposes, and of its place not only in the given dispositions of
high cultural provision in the city, but within the topographies and structures of a
modern consciousness. It is the first real moment, the last moment, and not a
moment too soon. It is a momentous business. Time is continuous, but the
turning of the millennium is taken to be of great and special significance: a
significant moment in the conceptual topographies and structures of cultural
space-time. (We measure out the lives of our civilizations in centuries.) It must be
marked; the mark signifying a measurement; measurement being a definition of
structure.

  We speak of entering the new century, of looking forward to it; of inhabiting it;
metaphors of our condition. No language without hidden metaphor; no
language that does not encapsulate myths. The museums of the last two centuries
(the Louvre was opened to the people—the first popular palace of art—201 years
ago) are the temples of their time: (Bankside was hailed as a temple of power):
they speak in the language of their time, encode the myths of their time. They are
beautiful and powerful myths: they will continue to live, but only if
comprehended within the new topographies and new structures of a truly
modern consciousness. New times demand new myths told in new languages.
New purposes renew old structures and redefine the dispositions of spaces on old
maps. Now is the moment for purposeful propositions.

'Sometimes I dream of a work of really great breadth, ranging through the whole region of element, object,
meaning and style.' Klee

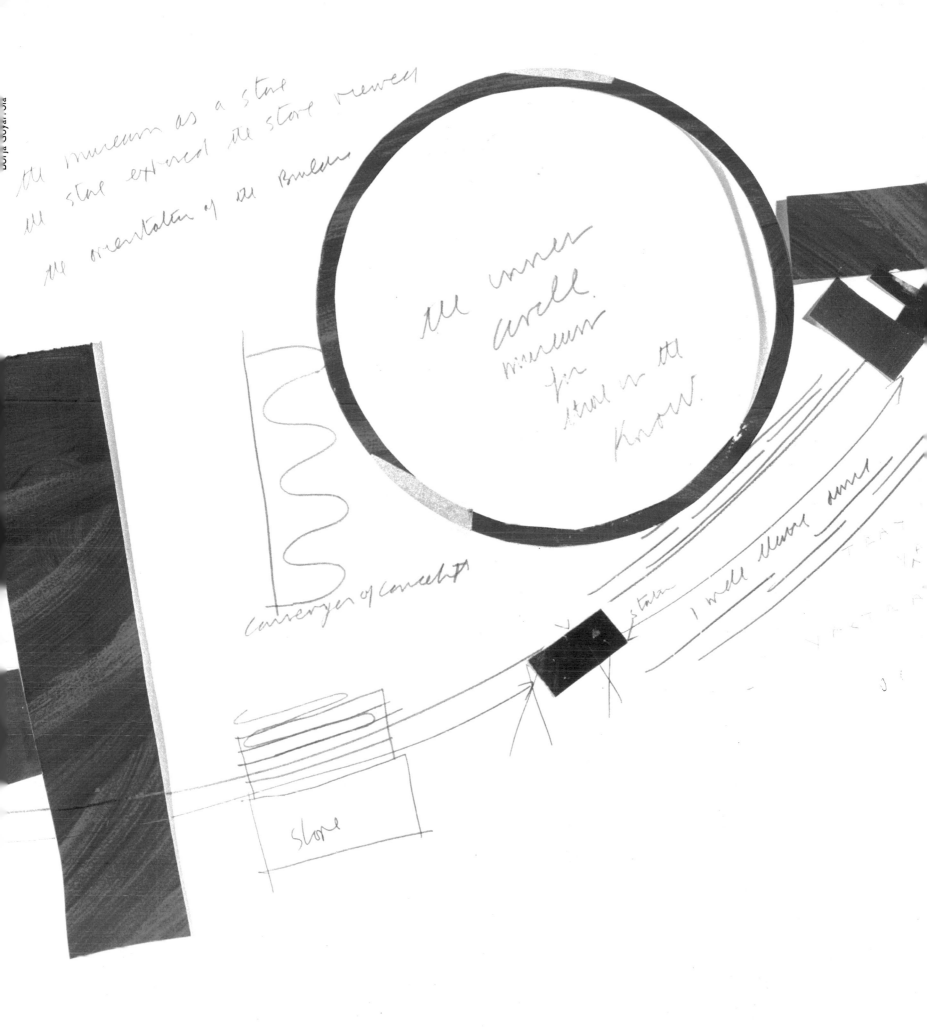

William Alsop   Mel Gooding   Bruce McLean   *April 1994*

PUTTING ART IN ITS PLACE

Putting Art in its Place is a series of five films directed by Maggie Ellis, funded by The Arts Council and Channel Four. The series focuses on art in the public domain – art which addresses contemporary issues in both the rural and urban context. 'Showcase City' focuses on Birming-ham's 'one percent for art' policy which has allowed it to commission new art works for public spaces. 'Changing Faces' looks at the problem of the dehumanising elements of urbanism and selects two examples of towns who have employed resident artists to bring new life to blighted areas. 'Gallery Without Walls' examines the reasons behind the success of the Yorkshire Sculpture Park which attracts half a million visitors a year. 'On Common Ground' analyses which ele-ments of rural and urban Britain should be preserved while 'Along the Tracks' examines the impact of art in the context of transport.

'Along the Tracks' provides an insight into one solution to the current drive for sustainability adopted by Sustrans (Sustainable Transport) an organisation founded in 1984 by, among others, the present director John Grimshaw. He saw the decline of the railways as an opportunity to create a national network of cycle paths. Cycling is an extremely appropriate method of travel for a small crowded and polluted world since it is relatively cheap, non-polluting, uses few materials, is widely available to young and old and enhances health and fitness.

Since 1980, Sustrans have constructed 250 miles of cycling routes linking towns and cities all over Britain. These continuous safe routes through the countryside use the existing bridges and tunnels as a way of crossing roads safely without any conflict with traffic. Some bridges are obsolete and traffic engineers see them as obstructions but the cyclists remember them as features in the journey. Grimshaw sites the Hown's Gill viaduct, on the path which runs eastwards from Consett to the coast at Sunderland, as the most wonderful structure in the whole of that district. The popularity of such architectural features combined with the demand for seating and watering places along these cycle routes, prompted a series of commissions for site specific 'sculpture' at intervals along the path.

Artists were asked to explore the history of the site or to relate it to the scenery. Seats designed by Jim Partridge and Liz Walmsley, are made from old railway sleepers and are positioned to look out over beautiful views. They function both as resting places and as bike racks and this design was so successful that it has been repeated for other paths around the country. Their strong effective designs can also be seen in various footbridges, shelters, seating and picnic benches around the country. The Gaius Sentius drinking fountain by Gordon Young was inspired by the Roman Centurion who is thought to have built the Roman road which bisects the Bristol and Bath Railway Path. The fountain is adjacent to a memorial to Gaius Sentius' wife from which Young adopted the Roman habit of allowing soldiers, untrained in carving, to inscribe the name of the sponsors into the stone. Young's light hearted 'Carry-on' film representation of the Roman general is aimed at amusing the children who are its most frequent visitors.

Andy Goldsworthy was commissioned to create two large-scale earthworks for the track from Consett to Sunderland. 'The Maze' at Leadgate echoes the shape of old mine workings several hundred feet below. Over a quarter of a mile long, it gave him the opportunity to make one of his largest works and is situated on the site of the former Eden Colliery which closed in 1980. Nothing can be built on this land because of the threat of subsidence caused by the 300 foot shaft

FROM ABOVE: Jim Partridge and Liz Walmsley, bench made of railway sleepers; Gordon Young, Gaius Sentius; Andy Goldsworthy, OPPOSITE FROM ABOVE: The Maze; Lambton Earthwork

below and so the site had become a rubbish tip. The maze is positioned beside a complex of roads and John Grimshaw describes it as a healing process, the rhythmic equivalent of a 'round about' solution. Maggie Ellis emphasises that many of these projects are seen as solutions to the use of land which seems to have no intrinsic value or potential for development. The Lambton Earthwork at Chester-Le-Street, is built on the site of a wide railway cutting on land which also has no planning value. The work starts narrow and ends wide giving a sense of direction – 'I wanted a feeling of movement of earth risen up and flowing – a river of earth'. Goldsworthy's serpentine form recalls the local legend of the Lambton Worm who reputedly terrorised the area feeding 'On caalves an' lambs an' sheep, An swally little bairns alive, When they laid doo te sleep'. Goldsworthy is adamant that he did not know of the legend when he designed the earthwork. He acknowledges that it has the qualities of snaking but that although it is not a snake, it has evolved through a similar response to the environment. 'The snake has evolved through a need to move close to the ground sometimes below sometimes above – it is an expression of the space it occupies. It is the way a river finds its route down a valley, the ridge of a mountain, the root of a tree . . . for me it is a potent recurring form in nature which I have explored through working in bracken, snow, sand, leaves, grass, trees, earth . . .'. After several small-scale experiments with this shape using sand and earth, he supervised Steve Fox the excavation operator who carved the shapes very precisely for both the Maze and the Lambton Earthwork.

David Gray, the Sustrans project manager in the North East agrees with the loose interpretation of the functional aspect of the brief. The function could be to draw attention to the history of the area or simply to provoke discussion and enquiry – in many cases the historical angle is attributed to a piece subsequent to its completion. Gray compares Richard Harris's work Kyo Undercurrent on the Annfield Plain in County Durham, to 'the bones of the earth . . . an anatomical drawing where the wind has exposed the structure suggesting activity beneath the surface'. Harris chose a sandhill which had been laid down by a glacier in the last ice age. The sculpture acts as a mediator between the track and the surrounding land since the earth and stone ramps edge back from the cycle track following an existing network of paths made by people crossing the common land. 'People are following the tops of the ramps as I hoped they would and as the grass isn't growing there so it is becoming defined. The structure of the site is being re-defined by people's movement, so there is another layer on top of what I put down, as well as what was there already.'

Other examples of this living sculpture can be seen in Ken Turnell's Flower Mine at Stanley in County Durham. This is an example of Gray's 'post-justification' theory where the earthwork is thought to commemorate a pit disaster on this, the site of the Louisa Pit where an accident caused the death of 100 boys and men. The actual derivation is that the seeds for ox eye daisies that Turnell had planned to plant on the mine were so expensive that he decided to collect the seeds from each flowering and replant – hence 'flower mine'. The image works from the visual principle of growth. The drawn image appears to increase in size from its centre and the seed actually travels and increases from this centre to its airborne surrounds. Another aspect of living local history is revealed through Sally Matthews 'Beamish Shorthorns' which are scrap metal sculptures of the traditional local breed of cows. She used the lane like quality of the track to evoke an image of cows wandering back from milking, docile and broody, moving slowly to graze the verges. She got scrap metal from the

FROM ABOVE: Richard Harris, Kyo Undercurrent; Ken Turnell, Flower Mine; Sally Matthews, Beamish Shorthorn

Consett yard which was a good equivalent for the strong bone structure of a cow. The colour of the rust is somewhat like the red roan of shorthorns.

Many of the works are pertinent to the industry of the area, whether it is the demise of the coal mining and steel making or its previous history as an agricultural area. David Kemp is an artist with an unusual sensitivity to place, he works in a narrative manner tapping veins of local history to weave legends around each site. Kemp recycled industrial materials to create his post industrial giant, King 'Coal' on Pelton Fell in Durham. The work is comprised of a giant fan impeller from the nearby Boldon Colliery, masonry from the Consett Railway Station Bridge, bricks from the demolished kilns at Templetown brick works and pit shovels from Wolsingham Iron Company. This narrative piece describes a metaphor between the closure of the Durham collieries and the demise of King Coal's power as he sinks back into the ground, leaving only his head exposed. Construction took five weeks, finishing coincidentally on the 15th October 1992, the date of the announced closures of the last pits in the Durham Coalfields. Sustrans encourages the use of local voluntary labour and Kemp's team comprised of those locals who were unemployed as a result of the closure of local industry.

Another example of Kemp's work can be found on the top of the Durham moors where the old railway cuts round the flank of Stoney Heap and which runs in a wide arc through Leadgate and on to Consett. Kemp's 'Heads for the Hills': the Ironmaster with his goggles and the Miner with his pit lamp and wheel, are reminiscent of the Easter Island heads both in their scale and presence. They look out over the great steel works at Consett which closed in 1980 and was subsequently levelled to the ground. The heads were built from the heaviest steel available, mainly 10 to 15 mm plate, are 20 feet high and weigh over 14 tons. Poems were written about the community that grew up as a result of the industry. Kemp has inscribed a rusting steel plate that he found beside the track with the legend of the old transformers – 'The men that live near here, dug in the ground for the black stone, in their giant huts they burnt the earth, they turned the sky red. A river of steel ran to the sea where it was transformed again into locomotives, ships and machines which transformed the world'. Kemp's giant steel figures serve as an emotive memorial to the works – he suggests that the transformer cases from which these sculptures are constructed were quite possibly those through which the current that powered the furnaces may have flowed.

With the Lost 17th, Kemp gives rein to his narrative imagination drawing on the profusion of Roman ruins surrounding this site, 17 miles out of Glasgow, to create an army made from oxygen bottles welded to rail saddles with railway spikes on top of their heads. The welding team consisted of unemployed workers on a 'training scheme'. Kemp dismissed this demeaning categorisation explaining that, for example one of them had been a Boiler maker and was therefore a superb welder since he had always had to weld under high pressure. Kemp concluded that if he had his time over again he would not have done the army of the Lost 17th but the army of the unemployed.

The sculptures stimulate cyclists and other users to question the artist's perception and interpretations, but most importantly they help to humanise a public space and encourage people to treat their environment with respect and care.

David Kemp, FROM ABOVE: King Coal; The Ironmaster; The Lost 17th.

Sustrans Head Office, 35 King Street, Bristol, BS1 4DZ. Tel: 0272 268893. Videos of the series 'Putting Art in its Place' can be obtained from Arts Council Films, 14 Great Peter Street, London SW1P 3NQ. Tel: 071 973 6454

URBAN PARADISE Gardens in the City

This event is designed to provide an artistic forum to encourage practical and theoretical ideas related to urban space and the garden in our inner cities. The exhibition represents the proposal stage in which artists present their garden designs in the form of drawings, photographs and maquettes. The Public Art Fund will then continue to facilitate design development and community involvement in order to 'create a realm where an artist's vision, a community's commitment and the government's co-operation will yield a public amenity of an enduring nature'.

Each artist has chosen to reveal a different meaning from the site. Meg Webster's practical design seeks to reinforce an understanding of the ground as a productive resource. The rhythmic quality of the spaces which open and close, rise and fall allows diverse characteristics from the garden, park, farm and city to be perceived as an integrated whole. Individual community garden plots are interwoven with ecological demonstrations of hedgerow, ponds, streams, and bogs, and further joined with production spaces of orchards and organic vegetable plots.

Vito Acconci concentrates less on the practical idea of gardening, and addresses the psychological significance of public and private spaces in the city through the temporary garden he has planned for the MetroTech Centre, Brooklyn. A horizontal plane of ivy, four feet above the ground is constructed using a system of horizontal chains covered in ivy spread slung between opposite sides of the perimeter fence. He claims that 'When you use the garden, you become "used" by the garden: you're wrapped up in the garden, surrounded by the garden . . . it is all around you, at chest-height. As you go inside, further and further, the garden comes closer and closer. When you sit down, the planting is at your head, over your head; you sink down inside the garden'.

Jeff Wall explores this theme further through the medium of photography, he captures intimate yet fictional moments in contemporary life revealing an intense psychology below the surface of his images. In his recent work *In the Public Garden*, he presents a thought provoking reversal of W Eugene Smith's romanticised and seminal work, *Walk to Paradise Garden* 1946. Wall's image contrasts the 'innocent pleasure' of Eugene Smith's child with an adult perception of public space as a sensory and visceral experience that may on occasion give rise to a disconcerting anxiety.

Justen Ladda approaches the 'psychological' from a surreal aspect, some would say a characteristically artistic angle. His design for the Fox Street Garden in the Bronx plays on the contradictory, combining elements from familiar compositions into an illusory form. For Ladda the difference between reality and fiction is only a matter of distance – a gap. He expresses this gap through a mountainous outcropping which will look as if an alpine slope suddenly appeared in this neat suburban area. From inside, the garden will be a place of refuge with paths leading through sunken spaces with views of only nature and sky. Spaces for picnicking, individual garden plots and a playground mean that despite its surreal appearance, the garden will become integrated within the community.

The necessarily contrived element in this surrealism can be compared to the human tendency to organise nature expressed by some of the other artists. *The Pull: Wild Gardens at Paerdegat* conceived by Lorna Jordan for the Paerdegat Basin, Brooklyn explores the balancing point between nature and human control

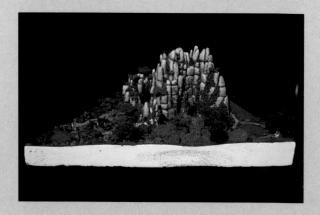

FROM ABOVE: Meg Webster & Philip Parker, model for Atlanta Garden, 1993; Vito Acconci, model of proposal for the MetroTech Centre,1994; Jeff Wall, In the Public Garden, 1993; Justen Ladda, model of proposal for the Fox Street Garden, 1994

addressing the human tendency to organise nature. A horse-shoe magnet acts as an observation deck and symbolises the desire to pull life back to the basin. The garden is designed around the magnet's lines of force, for example a series of tethered floating islands respond to the magnetism of the tides. A metaphor for the successive waves of peoples who have passed through this area is expressed as a series of smaller spaces conceived as metaphorical stepping stones. The shoreline of the tidal wetlands is curvilinear harbouring waterside gardens for canoeists.

Haim Steinbach's conceptual proposal highlights the cultural ritual of the city dweller and the window-box as a metaphor for human control over nature. He presents this concept through a garden comprised of a series of groves, small secluded gardens nestled within a proposed serpentine wall surrounding the Newtown Creek Wastewater Plant in Greenpoint Brooklyn. A secondary wall is proposed to hold treated water creating a moat between the two walls, water would then feed fountains, cooling the shaded gardens. The ensemble of mount and trees is separated from the street by this water boundary just as if it were in a flower pot. Through this 'artifice' Steinbach emphasises the inevitability of what is natural becoming cultivated and manicured in a city.

Each of these projects involves the local community in some way, whether in the design or the implementation of the garden, or in a more conceptual manner as can be seen in the Rosetta Garden in Fort Greene, Brooklyn, designed by Gary Simmons. Inspired by the controversy surrounding Martin Bernal's breakthrough study, *Black Athena*, the *Rosetta Garden* is a physical embodiment of Simmons' previous works erasing and reversing racial stereotypes. Four original sculptures in classical poses embody heroism of the everyday and refuse the empirical quest for legitimacy based on the identification of great historical figures descending from established racial lines. Like the Rosetta Stone itself, the garden translates between the classical past and cultural present. Its contrasting materials comment on the romantic relationship to antiquity: rose bushes and grape arbours conjure images of romance and hedonism; concrete seating and brick facing recall the austere materials of the city surrounding. Together, these materials question the calls for authoritarian control of our youth and instead promote the bacchanalian celebration of culture and identity-making.

Gilbert Boyer provides another interpretation of the multicultural context of these gardens in his design planned for Peretz Square, Lower East Side, Manhattan. Boyer's garden is named after the work of the seminal Yiddish and Hebrew poet Isaac Peretz, *The Garden of Babel – Leaves and Lives*. The garden is designed to mirror Peretz's interest in gathering the stories of ordinary people to a poetic end. The Babel-like diversity of cultures, ethnic groups and languages in this area is represented through texts in many languages carved on irregular slabs of granite which wind through a tapestry of cement, asphalt and cobblestones. The only designed vegetation will be trees but in the summer, ivy will grow over the granite stones obscuring the inscriptions. Seasonal changes mean that only one of the gardens will be evident and the other remembered at any one time.

Visions of Urban Paradise at PaineWebber Art Gallery, New York 14 April – 1 July 1994

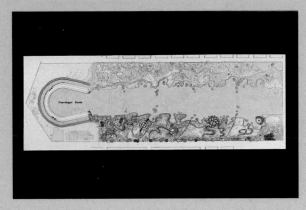

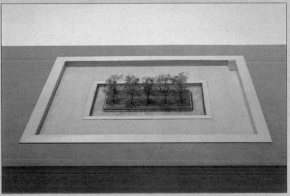

FROM ABOVE: Lorna Jordan, The Pull: Wild Gardens at Paerdeqat, 1994; Haim Steinbach, model for Grove (Recessed Planter A); Gary Simmons, Rosetta Garden; Gilbert Boyer, The Garden of Babel – Leaves and Lives

JIM BUCKLEY – Flood

Meiho is in a mountainous region south of the Japanese Alps. Artists were invited to select locations within the town and region to produce temporary works. The abandoned fish farm I chose was easily visible to both motorists and pedestrians from a bridge spanning the gorge and fast-flowing mountain river. The only continuous sound was of a large waterfall. The fish farm lies below the bridge which forms part of the main road through the town.

This site suggested to me reclamation. The cultural significance of the fish pervades Japanese life, and this appeared as a natural vehicle through which to realise the work. By altering slightly the given characteristics of the site and considering the Japanese tendency to replace rather than to renew, I focused on a site which was set apart from the daily activity of the town. Its location afforded it visibility, separation, serenity, abandonment and isolation.

On the overgrown site, I chose seven of the fish tanks. These were first cleaned of vegetation, washed and painted. The water flow system was re-activated, resulting in a continuous flow of water moving through the tanks. A lighting system was installed, run off a generator for two hours each night beginning at dusk.

Flood was originally intended to be a temporary work. However, it was so well received by local people, greeted with an ovation when first turned on, that the Town Council in conjunction with the landowner have decided to make the work permanent. The lighting system has been connected to the street lighting power supply so that the work is turned on at dusk and off at dawn, automatically.

ANDY GOLDSWORTHY

'I have a social and intellectual need to make photographs. As Brancusi said, "Why talk about my sculpture when I can photograph it". Photography is my way of talking, writing and thinking about my art'.
The launch of Andy Goldsworthy's latest book, STONE, forces us to consider the controversial but necessary relationship with photography that the eco-artist movement's transient, site-specific work demands. 'The photograph does not replace but comes out of the working process and can be as much part of an artist's vocabulary as recorded sound is of a musician's. The photograph is incomplete. The viewer is drawn into the space between the image and work. A bridge needs to be made between the two. It is necessary to know what is like to get wet, feel a cold wind, touch a leaf, throw stones, compress snow, suck icicles . . . often reaching back into childhood to when those experiences were more alive. If the photograph were to become so real that it overpowered and replaced the work outside then it would have no purpose or meaning in my art'. So which is, in fact, the work of art, the photograph or that which is photographed? *Seven holes Canonbury clay dug from outside the back door several months in drying* was installed inside the Greenpeace UK Office, London while the only record of the graceful arc of *Wet sand cupped, squeezed, thrown out of the water*, in Lake Michigan is a picture taken by Judith Goldsworthy. The first is as permanent (though changing) and geographically accessible as such works of art can be but, while the second is a moment captured on film, it is possible that neither the artist or photographer were able to grasp the original image with the naked eye. Whether we decide that the contrast between the solid accessibility of the first and the mobile ephemeral nature of the second comment on the concept of the integrity of an art work, we must remember that by showing us the spectrum of possibile interpretations of the natural world, Andy Goldsworthy's work becomes a genuine reflection of the unique diversity therein.

Stone by Andy Goldsworthy, Viking, 1994, 120pp, colour ills, HB £35. Three London exhibitions coincide with this publication: Scaur Water Stone, The Grob Gallery, 21 April-27 May; Hanging Stone, Michael Hue-Williams Fine Art, 21 April-27 May; Herd of Arches, 27 Old Bond Street, 21 April-27 May and exhibitions in Tokyo, San Francisco and Paris.

FROM ABOVE: Yellow elm leaves laid over a rock low water; Wet sand cupped, squeezed thrown out of water; BACKGROUND: Seven holes Canonbury clay dug from outside the back door several months in drying

JAMES HUGONIN

James Hugonin moved to Northumberland because of the particular quality of light and because he feels that there's 'an openness about it, room to breathe'. The quality of 'being in a place' and 'being absorbed' by light and colour is very important to him. His minimalist technique is influenced by a Seurat exhibition he saw in Paris in 1991; 'the tenderness with which the paintings were made which seemed to imbue the images with light'. He has also gleaned ideas from the work of the American artists Agnes Martin and Brice Marden – the former employed a grid structure and the latter a colour field technique. Hugonin's repetitive use of a grid evolved from a desire to make the statement more intense by reintroducing detail without being decorative. 'Some people think the grid's a constriction, but I believe if I use it inventively it gives me incredible freedom'. He concentrates on different paint textures using one colour at a time and using his hand span as the gauge to achieve a rhythm, focusing on the way light shifts and moves across the land-scape. 'I feel such a strong pull from what is outside. I've never actually wanted to paint landscapes; it isn't to do with represen-tation, it's about how it's possible to best reflect the shifting quality of light.' (Extract from *Briggflats*, Parts 1 to 4, 1987) *'Paintings 1983-1993', Mappin Art Gallery, Sheffield, 19 Feb-27 March 1994*

SONG OF THE EARTH

During the last 25 years a generation of Northern European artists has gained prominence by creating art which reflects their experience of the natural world. Fascinated with nature's materials and processes these artists make sculpture, but favour selection, collection, rearrangement and documentation rather than traditional fabrication.

Differing from the American Land Movement, these European artists do not alter the natural environment with monumental earthworks, rather they select from what nature has to offer. Natural phenomena, therefore, have more of a direct effect on their work than they have on nature.

A small selection of artists has been invited to participate in the exhibition 'Song of the Earth', chosen to represent some of the most powerful approaches to this complex subject. They include Roger Ackling, Chris Drury, Wolfgang Laib, Nikolaus Lang and Herman de Vries. A series of conferences and discus-sions have been organised to promote a greater awareness of the natural environment and our relationship to it, challenging the distinction between art and science.
'Song of the Earth' is a National Touring Exhibition starting at the Royal Botanic Garden, Edinburgh, 29 July-10 Sept 1995

Chris Drury, Cloud Chamber

JEAN-LUC VILMOUTH – Channel Fish

Jean-Luc Vilmouth's transformation of the Waterloo International Terminal into a gigantic aquarium through his permanent installation, Channel Fish, for European Passenger Services, signifies a new relationship between artwork and site. A visual metaphor inspired by the function and form of the building, the Vilmouth shoal of fish heightens the technical brilliance and organic qualities of Nicholas Grimshaw's grand project. Articulated and motorised, the ten lançons or sandeels (fished in the Channel at full moon) respond to the departure of the new Eurostar trains bound for Paris and Brussels.

   In Summer 1992, the client, European Passenger Services, Nicholas Grimshaw and the advisory architects, Levitt Bernstein, decided to commission an important work of art for the building, and invited the non-profit consultants Public Art Commissions Agency to organise a competition. Over 80 artists were considered and Vilmouth's proposal was unanimously selected in September 1993. In addition to European Passenger Services' principal sponsorship, the commission is supported with an Association of Business Sponsorship of the Arts, Business Sponsorship Incentive Scheme award, the Henry Moore Foundation, the Arts Council of England, and the French Embassy/Association Française d'Action Artistique. The work will be installed in September 1994. *(Vivien Lovell)*

ROGER ACKLING

Years ago, Roger Ackling ceased doing 'drawings' on card because these required frames which someone else had to make. Holding a simple magnifying lens to focus sunlight on small pieces of found wood, he burns the surface with horizontal rows of dots. Blackened lines may cover front and side surfaces while other areas are deliberately untouched. Focused on these lines, Ackling becomes one with his surroundings. 'When I'm working and lose concentration I imagine that the wood becomes a landscape, a great space . . . I'm travelling over a fantastically huge space . . . and that helps me enjoy [making] the piece.' Despite this feeling of immense scale, the geography of Ackling's work is not representative – it grows as he scorches fresh lines, each mark is a self-portrait of its source, ciphers in unconscious codes. The character of the marks is born of a season, a time of day, the vagaries of local weather – quite as much as from the artist's mood or the dryness of the wood. Roger Ackling's work is both modest and direct – salvaging wood fragments already shaped by man or machine, employing solar energy in its purest form, his sculpture comes and goes without intrusion, save the wisps of smoke thrown off by each tiny crater as it chars.
'Flooded Margins' Annely Juda Fine Art, London, 12 May-25 June 1994

Weybourne 'Sol', 1992

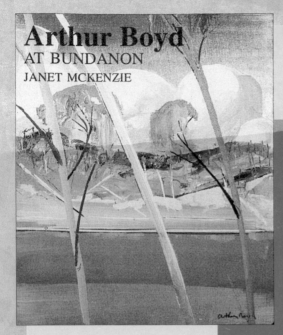

*A*rthur Boyd is Australia's most famous and prolific 20th-century artist, and with 25,000 works of art in numerous collections, his paintings, graphics and ceramics are an established and substantial part of Australia's art legacy. In 1993, he gave his favourite workplace, Bundanon, on the Shoalhaven River in New South Wales, to the nation, where the Australian government plans to create a major art centre. The relationship between the landscape of the Shoalhaven River and Arthur Boyd's artistic career is of interest to artists and laymen alike. Boyd's concerns go beyond the landscape to the future of our environment and the exploration of human vulnerability and folly, of death and destruction. With the help of the National Gallery of Australia and Arthur Boyd himself, Janet McKenzie has researched and analysed the artist's work realised at, and inspired by, Bundanon.

The final chapter deals with the future of Bundanon with architectural schemes for the building of the new art centre by Will Alsop and Michael Spens.

PB ISBN: 1 85490 338 1 £19.95
305 x 252mm, 128 pages
140 illustrations, mainly in colour
Publication: June 1994

*T*he elements of landscape design are explored with clear, detailed drawings which convey exactly the effect of formal, climatic, geological, textural and architectural botanical elements and their significance for the landscape designer.

This is the first comprehensive study of all the various elements that go to make up the vocabulary of landscape architecture; hard landscape (pavings, squares, steps and walls) and soft landscape (paths, tree planting and hedges, for example) and the numerous devices (vistas, walkways and clearings) to be deployed. The ways in which water (lakes, pools, rills, cascades and canals) can be utilised to effect are also categorised clearly and in a comprehensible manner.

Schaal sets out to relate historical methods of landscape design to contemporary ideas in art and design with a lucid descriptive text that students, teachers and practitioners alike will find highly inspirational as well as of direct practical value. Sir Geoffrey Jellicoe provides a valuable introduction.

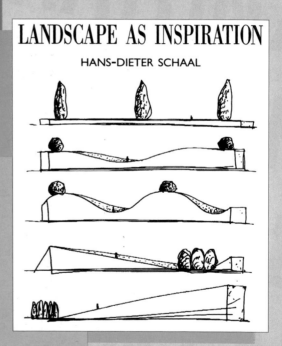

PB ISBN: 1 85490 303 9 £39.95
240 x 280mm, 384 pages
400 b/w illustrations,
Publication: April 1994

Further information can be obtained from Academy Group Ltd 071 402 2141

ART AND THE
NATURAL ENVIRONMENT

The Boyle Family, Street Study with three drains and a yellow parking line, *painted fibreglass, 1987*

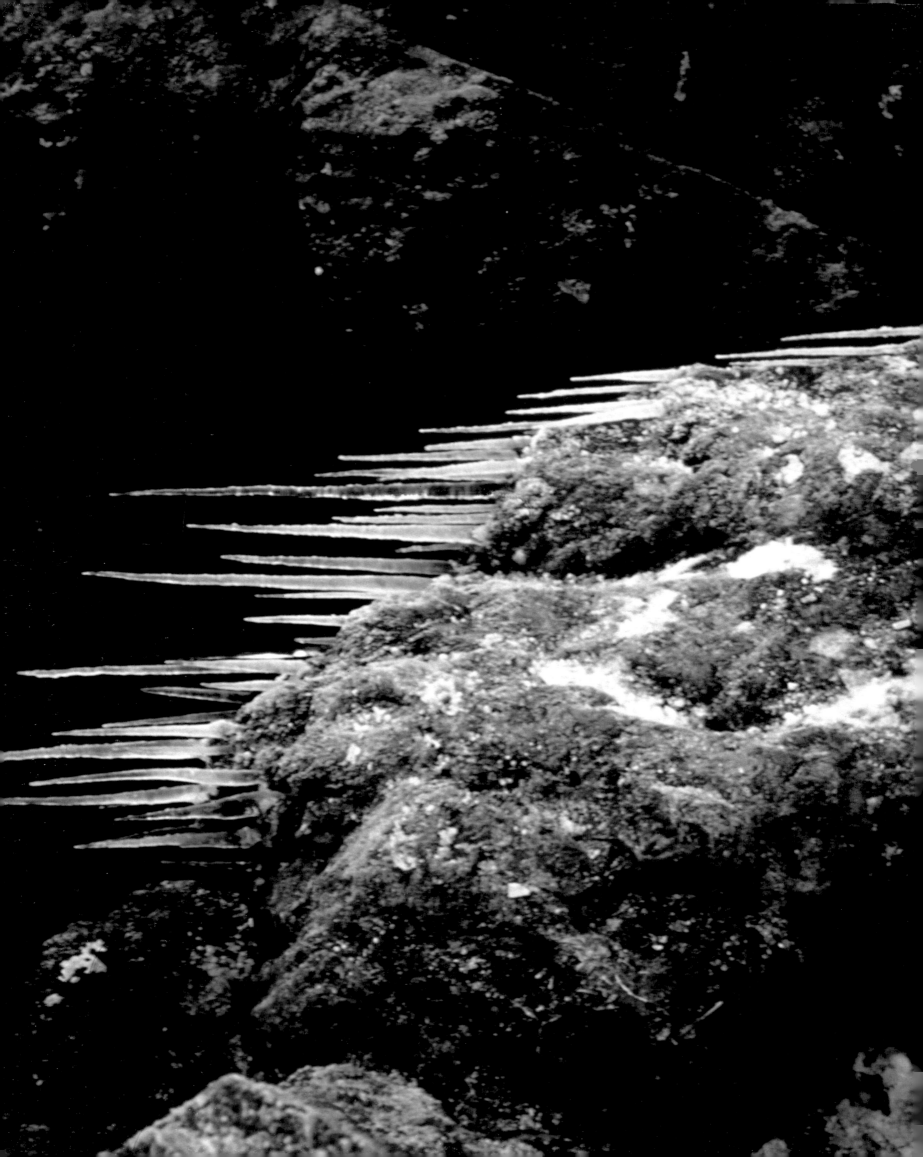

Art & Design

ART AND THE
NATURAL ENVIRONMENT

ABOVE: David Nash, Charred Cross Egg, 1994, oak, 178x93cm (diameter), courtesy Annely Juda Fine Art, London;
OPPOSITE: Andy Goldsworthy, Icicles frozen to rock, Scaur Water, Dumfriesshire, Jan 1991,
from Andy Goldsworthy, Stone, Viking, London, 1994

ACADEMY EDITIONS • LONDON

Acknowledgements

We would like to thank the contributors to *Art and the Natural Environment* for their advice, interest and support, all of whom made this issue of *Art & Design* both fascinating and a pleasure to compile.

The Survival of Culture and Nature *pp6-15* images courtesy the following individuals and galleries, *p6* © Dia Center for the Arts, *p8 from above* © Hans Haacke, Ronald Feldman Fine Arts, New York, Agnes Denes, *p11 from above* John Weber Gallery, New York, Alan Sonfist, John Weber Gallery, James Turrell, *p12 from above* © Christo, Patricia Johanson, *p14* Jyoti Duwadi and Barbara C Matilsky; **Re-spect** *pp16-23, p16* Ronald Feldman Fine Arts, New York, *pp18-23* Institut pour l'Art et la Ville, Givors; **Wolfgang Laib** *pp24-31* images courtesy the artist; **TICKON** *pp32-61* compiled by Alfio Bonanno and Gertrud Købke Sutton, all photographs unless otherwise mentioned were taken by Alfio Bonanno, the Nils Udo piece was translated from German by Leonore Stuart; **Giuliano Mauri** *pp62-67* first published in Vittorio Fagone, *Giuliano Mauri: Arte nella natura 1981-1993*, Mazzotta, 1993, images courtesy the artist; **David Nash** *pp68-73* text first published in *David Nash*, Kunsthallen, Brandts Klædefabrik, Odense, exhib cat, 1993, *p68* photos by Alfio Bonanno, images courtesy Annely Juda Fine Art, London; **'Birds'** *pp74-79, p74* courtesy Lynne Hull; **This Rock, This Street, This Earth** *pp80-83* images courtesy The Boyle Family; **Ian Hamilton-Finlay** *pp84-93* images courtesy the artist; **Acer Pseudoplatanus** *pp94-96* photographs by Edward Woodman, courtesy Michael Petry.

Notes on Contributors

Barbara C Matilsky has written extensively on art and nature, in 1992 she curated and wrote the accompanying volume (Rizzoli) for the show 'Fragile Ecologies: Artists' Interpretations and Solutions', the Queens Museum of Art, New York. **Amanda Crabtree** was project co-ordinator at the Maison du Rhône, Institut pour l'Art et La Ville, she is now working at Le Fresnoy, Studio Nationale des Arts Contemporains, France. **Clare Farrow** guest-edited *Parallel Structures: Art, Dance, Music*, A&D 11/12 93, she is a freelance writer and editor based in London. **Alfio Bonanno** is an artist and founder of TICKON (Tranekaer Internationale Centre for Kunst Og Natur), he lives on Langeland in Denmark. **Gertrud Købke Sutton** is an art-critic, curator and writer based in Denmark, she is Vice-Chairman of AICA (Association International de Critiques d'Art) and also of TICKON. **Vittorio Fagone** is a contemporary art critic and historian, joint responsible for the project 'Art in Nature' which documents artists' work in the environmental field, he is currently Director of the Galleria d'Arte Moderna e Contemporanea – Accademia Carrara di Bergamo. **David Reason** is Senior Lecturer in Interdisciplinary Studies and Head of Psychoanalytic Studies at the University of Kent, his publications on land art include major essays on the work of Hamish Fulton, *The Unpainted Landscape*, Coracle Press and *An Art Touching Nature* Thames & Hudson (forthcoming). **Mark Boyle** is an artist and co-founder of the Boyle Family, he is based in London. **Paul Crowther** guest-edited *New Art from Eastern Europe: Identity and Conflict*, A&D 3/4 94, he is lecturer in art history at the University of St Andrews, Scotland, his most recent book is *Art and Embodiment: From Aesthetics to Self-Consciousness*, Clarendon Press. **Michael Petry** is an artist and co-founder of Museum of Installation, London, he is co-author of *Installation Art*, Thames & Hudson, 1994.

COVER: Nils Udo, Red Beech with Rowanberries, *1993, photo Nils Udo*
INSIDE FRONT AND BACK COVERS: Mierle Laderman Ukeles, Glasphalt test for Danehy Park landfill project,
Cambridge MA, Asphalt plant, Brooklyn, 1993, Ronald Feldman Fine Arts, New York; BACK COVER: Giuliano Mauri, sketch

HOUSE EDITOR: Nicola Hodges EDITORIAL: Ramona Khambatta
ART EDITOR: Andrea Bettella CHIEF DESIGNER: Mario Bettella DESIGNER: Jason Rigby

First published in Great Britain in 1994 by *Art & Design* an imprint of the
ACADEMY GROUP LTD, 42 LEINSTER GARDENS, LONDON W2 3AN
MEMBER OF THE VCH PUBLISHING GROUP

ISBN: 1 85490 219 9

Contents

Mierle Laderman Ukeles, 100-ton cobalt-blue diamond of recycled glass,
from Re-spect, Givors, October 1993, photo Herve Hugues

ART & DESIGN PROFILE No 36

ART AND THE
NATURAL ENVIRONMENT

BARBARA C MATILSKY

THE SURVIVAL OF CULTURE AND NATURE
Perspectives on the History of Environmental Art

Through the ages, as humans altered their environment, achieving harmony with nature became critical for survival. The earliest artists appropriated images from the natural world to express its regenerative powers. Artworks were not conceived as isolated objects – as defined by modern Western values – but part of rituals that spiritually mediated a balance between people and nature. The cultures that emerged from this intimate relationship became the cornerstones of a society's identity. Consequently, the environmental degradation that today threatens biodiversity also results in the disappearance of a varied and distinguished cultural life that once flourished on this earth.

By challenging traditional Western concepts of art and nature and looking to ancient and indigenous traditions for inspiration, artists are perfectly positioned to help counter the crisis. This article interprets the environmental art of the United States as a catalyst for renewing an essential connection between humans and nature. Within this diverse movement, I will undertake to trace the evolution of ecological art, which creatively remediates land and water in or near major cities.[1]

Environmental destruction is no longer a regional, but a world-wide phenomenon. Nature's complex and far-reaching interactions reflect the planet's integrity as a living entity. Recognising this reality, the article concludes by envisioning the future of ecological art within a global context.

Environmental art, which encompasses ecological art, emerged during the late 1960s and early 1970s, a time of great social and political turmoil. It was a period of intense soul searching and questioning of traditional Western values and social relationships. People challenged the war in Vietnam, racial segregation and women's role in society, among a whole host of other issues. In addition to participating in this idealistic transformation of society, artists sought to infuse new meaning into their work.

Environmental art was one of a number of movements, including process, minimal and conceptual art, that addressed the notion of art as a static, isolated object to be exhibited in an enclosed gallery space. Artists sought to break out of the confinement and isolation of their studios which physically and conceptually limited their creative possibilities. Working with unconventional materials, they elevated process itself to the status of art.

To many artists, the urban scene and its powerful, controlling art market represented 'the establishment', while nature embodied and inspired the freedom to forge new directions in their work. For the first time since prehistoric peoples created earth and rock mounds and petroglyphs, large numbers of Western artists began making art in, and from, the landscape, reinterpreting elements and processes of nature indoors. Art and life hence became entwined.

As the entire art world was undergoing revolutionary change, so too was the way in which people perceived the environment. No longer were citizens willing to accept the harmful consequences of unlimited growth. They began reexamining the processes of industrialisation and their effects on nature and the quality of life. In 1962, Rachel Carson, a marine biologist, published *Silent Spring*, an account of how DDT and other synthetic pesticides jeopardise the health and ultimate survival of all living things. This book helped to mobilise the modern environmental movement.

In reaction to the exploitation of natural resources that left pollution in its wake, activists in Europe and the United States forced the passage of important pieces of regulatory legislation, including the US Clean Air Act of 1963. The impetus to use the judicial system in order to effect environmental change encouraged the formation of organisations like the Environmental Defense Fund, founded in 1967. As an alternative, environmentalists in 1969 established Greenpeace, which uses civil disobedience to influence and rally public opinion.

A significant event united the world in that year; television viewers were awed by the image of Earth from space. Earthrise from the moon magnified the beauty, fragility and finite aspects of the planet. The events of the decade culminated in the first Earth Day celebration in 1970 as millions of people expressed their concern for the fate of the world.

Environmental art is part of a long tradition whereby artists creatively respond to extreme environmental changes by introducing new art forms. Paleolithic artist-shamans may have created cave paintings to establish harmony between man and animals as climatic conditions

OPPOSITE: Walter de Maria, The Lightning Field, 1977, Albuquerque, New Mexico, photo John Cliett

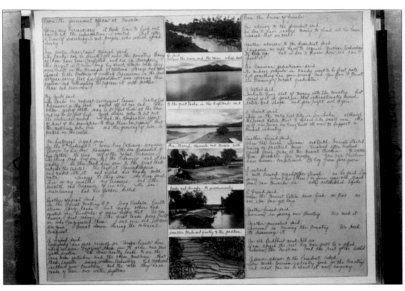

FROM ABOVE: Hans Haacke, Grass Grows, *1969, earth, winter and annual rye grass, installation at the Andrew Dickson White Museum, Cornell University, Ithica, New York; Helen Mayer Harrison and Newton Harrison, The Lagoon Cycle: Sixth Lagoon, panel 5 from* The Book of the Lagoons, *1972-82, hand-coloured sepia-toned photographs and text; Agnes Denes,* Wheatfield – A Confrontation, *2 acres of wheat planted and harvested, Battery Park Landfill, Downtown Manhattan, New York, Summer 1982, photo Agnes Denes; With artist in the field, photo John McGrail*

and overkilling threatened species fundamental to their survival. With the advent of intensive agriculture that gave rise to the great civilisations in the Middle East, Southeast Asia, the Indus Valley and Mesoamerica, artists reacted to deforestation and soil erosion by appropriating the image of the sacred tree into their work, symbolising fertility and regeneration. The emergence of landscape painting can be understood within the context of expanding urbanism that separated people from the natural world. Finally, the pinnacle of landscape painting in Europe and the United States, during the 19th century, coincides with the industrial revolution, when large areas of nature were developed and cities absorbed the population explosion.

Environmental art is multi-directional movement that embraces many currents, including ecological art. Beginning in the late 1960s, artists explored the seemingly infinite number of ways that nature could be interpreted. No longer were their materials and media limited to canvas and paint, stone, clay and wood. These artists experimented with radically new ways of interpreting the natural world – its fragility, power, processes, textures and the essence of site. They also wanted to change perceptions of art and nature by framing and magnifying both innovatively. Some artists were interested in communicating the totality of nature's interrelationships and through ecological art, proposed solutions to environmental problems. What united all of these artists was their emergence from the studio and their direct engagement with the natural world.

One aspect of environmental art is how it continuously changes as it responds to life's cycles and rhythms. Nature sometimes determines the form and content of a work. Once completed, the piece continues to evolve in tandem with natural processes. As a result, art and nature merge and become indistinguishable from each other. This is particularly true of artworks that interpret the processes of growth through the planting of grasses and trees. These early investigations provide one of the foundations for ecological art, which centres on the physical revitalisation of the environment.

One of the first artists to focus on natural processes was Hans Haacke, who grew grass on a three-foot square plexiglas cube at the Howard Wise Gallery, New York in 1966. Three years later, he expanded this organic concept in an exhibition called 'Earth Art' at the Andrew Dickson White Museum at Cornell University, Ithaca, New York. Here, the artist seeded a small mound of earth and grew winter rye grass. His simple title, *Grass Grows*, aptly described his subject which was the growth process itself. By bringing into the gallery and spotlighting an activity normally associated with the outdoors, Haacke enabled the public to closely scrutinise a fundamental process upon which all life depends.

By contrast, Agnes Denes' *Wheatfield, Battery Park City – A Confrontation (1982)* was dramatically sited outdoors in New York City. The artist temporarily transformed a debris-strewn, Manhattan landfill into a two-acre field that conveyed the sheer beauty and wonder of growth and cultivation to an urban population. After clearing the land, 225 truckloads of earth were brought in as topsoil. The artist created an irrigation system and maintained the field for four months. In August, one thousand pounds of grain were harvested. By creating an artwork with wheat, a staple food around the world, Denes also called attention to the issue of hunger. The juxtaposition of the wheatfield, silhouetted against the skyline of the World Trade Center, underlined the separation between country and city life which came together for a brief interlude in this work.

The concern for nurturing life was also dramatised by Helen and Newton Harrison in their performance piece titled *Making Earth*, 1970, which was reenacted at Artpark, Lewiston, New York in 1977. It consciously evokes ritual, an interaction that bonds people to communities and the natural world. When the artists actually made fertile earth from its elemental components, they were celebrating a life-sustaining mixture and responding to the depletion of top soil by insensitive agriculturists.

The Harrisons experimentally raised Sri Lankan crabs, in an artificial ecosystem to develop an inexpensive food source for the world's rising populations in *The First Lagoon*, 1972. Over the course of ten years, this work burgeoned into *The Lagoon Cycle* which addresses large, complex ecosystems. Through photography and poetic text, the artists contrast the damming of the Colorado River with the ecologically-sound, indigenous solutions to irrigation agriculture developed in Sri Lankan communities.

Since 1977, the Harrisons have investigated various aspects of watersheds and proposed solutions to maintain their delicate balance. In *Breathing Space for the Sava River, Yugoslavia*, 1988-90, they traced the course of this river ecosystem, one of Europe's last great flood plains. To safeguard a nature reserve, the Harrisons proposed making swamps along the drainage ditches entering the reserve and using plants as a natural purification system to eliminate pollutants. This work was conceived as a catalyst for public awareness and action. Most recently, their *Serpentine Lattice*, 1993, responds to the destruction of old growth forests in the Pacific Northwest of America by addressing the linkages of watersheds, rivers and forests.

The ecology of forests has been a concern of many artists, including Alan Sonfist. In the mid 1960s, he developed the concept of the *Time Landscape*, a plan to return areas of cities to their

FROM ABOVE: Nancy Holt, Sun Tunnels, 1973-76, Lucin, Utah, total lengths: 26.3m, tunnels: 5.5m, Sunset Summer Solstice, detail; Alan Sonfist, Time Landscape: Greenwich Village, 1965, native trees, shrubs, wild flowers; Robert Smithson, Spiral Jetty, April 1970, rocks, earth, salt crystals, photo Gianfranco Gorgoni; James Turrell, Roden Crater Project, Arizona, 1972-present (aerial view)

natural state. It is based on the belief that nature deserves to be resurrected and commemorated in much the same way as the heroes and events that have shaped human history. For *Time Landscape: Greenwich Village*, planted in 1978, Sonfist recreated a small native forest approximating the one that existed on the same Manhattan site prior to the arrival of European settlers. A once-vacant lot filled with garbage has become a living artwork, a monument to nature's powers of regeneration. For many visitors and residents, *Time Landscape* signals the arrival of the seasons and this sense of continuity within an urban matrix affirms the value of natural and social communities.

The idea of revitalising the city through environmental remediation art was conveyed in a series of visionary drawings by Patricia Johanson in 1969. They offer solutions to urban problems while providing habitat for plants and animals. Her *Garden Cities: Turtle Mound*, transforms a garbage landfill into a park shaped like a box turtle. The patterning of its shell inspires the design for 'gardens within gardens' and paths for people to examine and experience other forms of life. Although never realised, Johanson's concept is one of the first put forth by a contemporary artist to reclaim a landfill, a territory that has recently provided artists with fertile ground to execute their ideas.

This work became the foundation for the *Leonhardt Lagoon*, 1981-86, in Dallas, Texas. This once-polluted body of water is now a place where urban dwellers can walk along sculptured pathways to explore closely microhabitats for birds, fish, insects, and turtles. By reintroducing native plants and animals and balancing the lagoon's food chain, Johanson conserves a wetland and raises public awareness of this disappearing habitat.

In contrast to Johanson's ecological art that revitalises habitats, Robert Smithson approached nature differently. His *Spiral Jetty* was among the first large-scale, outdoor environmental projects called 'earthworks'. Sited in the waters of the Great Salt Lake, Utah, the jetty is constructed from 6,650 tons of rock and shaped into one of nature's most universal designs. The interweaving of land and water is visually striking, reflecting Smithson's interest in dual processes: 'growth, in the form of the crystallisation of salt on the jetty's rocks; and entropy, the slow and steady disintegration of systems, symbolised by the counterclockwise whirl of the jetty'.[2] The *Spiral Jetty*, submerged by rising waters soon after completion, has only recently resurfaced with its rocks encrusted with salt crystals as the artist envisioned.

Variations on the spiral became the basis for Smithson's many earth art-land reclamation proposals. In 1971, the artist formally introduced the philosophy behind such projects in his writings. Here, Smithson expressed the need for artists to take an active role in society and to integrate art into life. In 1972, he targeted land devastated by strip mining and offered his services to such mining companies as Kennecott Copper Corporation, US Steel and Union Carbide. He was not interested in creating artworks that rejuvenated the landscape, because he felt – as his wife, the artist Nancy Holt, pointed out – that such works cosmetically camouflage the damage. Earthworks were envisioned as a means of remediating sites through aesthetic manipulations of land and not by restoring habitats.

Working in abandoned or abused industrial areas raised a number of challenging issues for environmental artists. Many viewed strip-mine-reclamation art with scepticism, fearful that art would be used for corporate publicity and image promotion. Artists also believed that their involvement might absolve the company from fulfilling its responsibility to restore the land. These ethical questions were first publicly addressed by Robert Morris in a symposium to inaugurate the exhibition, 'Earthworks: Land Reclamation as Sculpture', at the Seattle Art Museum in 1979.[3]

More recent works like Nancy Holt's *Sky Mound*, 1988-present, located in New Jersey, demonstrate that an artist, collaborating with engineers and landscape architects, can potentially reclaim a 57-acre landfill into a socially useful place. Her plan for a public park provides for a naked-eye observatory and habitat for plants and migratory birds. At carefully calculated locations on the site, earth mounds and steel poles will be placed to align our vision with the sun rising and setting on the equinoxes and solstices. Like Smithson, she does not camouflage what this mound is, but purposely melds the vocabulary of art and the vernacular of landfill construction. *Sky Mound* evolves from her *Sun Tunnels*, constructed in 1973-76, which also enables visitors to experience the stars in the remote Utah desert.

Many other artists have sited their work in the desert, an environment that nurtures spiritual enlightenment by providing communion with nature in the wild. Here, James Turrell in his *Roden Crater*, 1972-present, located in Arizona, can dramatically focus and magnify the energies of light. By building earth rooms within and alongside the cone and excavating the crater to align these spaces with the sun and certain stars, he creates a site for people to experience seasonal solstices and celestial events as ancient peoples once did.

The isolation of site, which stimulates meditation and oneness with nature, is an important aspect of Walter de Maria's *Lightning Field*, 1974-77, located in the New Mexican desert. Using an array of stainless steel poles – 400 poles extend

FROM ABOVE: Christo, Running Fence, 1972-76, Sonoma and Marin Counties, California, 5.8m x 40km, photos Jeanne-Claude Christo; Patricia Johanson, Leonhardt Lagoon, 1981-86, Dallas, Texas, view of Saggitaria Platyphylla (Delta Duck Potato), gunite, plants and animals, 71.6 x 53.3 x 3.6m; View of Pteris Multifida (Texas Fern), gunite, plants and animals, 68.6 x 34 x 3.6m east-west for one mile and north-south for one kilometre – De Maria measures and frames space within a vast panorama. The work presents a focal point whereby viewer's can appreciate the changing effects of light upon land and sculpture. Because of its remoteness, one consciously makes a pilgrimage to the site to experience the art and one of the ultimate expressions of nature's power – lightning.

Many of Christo's environmental artworks measure and interpret the breadth and distances of nature by delineating the contours of the land. In *Running Fence, Sonoma and Marin Counties*, 1972-76, he created a sculpture of steel poles and nylon fabric that snaked across 24.5 miles of Northern California farmland for two weeks. These man-made materials enhanced the landscape's forms, colours and textures. By reflecting light at various times of day, the sculpture dramatised changing atmospheric conditions. The land functioned as a giant canvas and the sun's glow directly provided a palette of shifting tonalities.

The long, painstaking process of creating such works – the negotiations with land holders, meetings with public officials, engineers and manufacturers, filing of environmental impact statements and the sale of Christo's own works through which the project is funded – is as essential and artful as the natural processes reflected by the work itself. Most importantly, Christo brings local people into the creative process of making art and alters their perceptions of both art and nature by highlighting their physical beauty. *Running Fence* became an event with large numbers of people involved in its execution. The work was as much performance as it was sculpture.

Performance is an effective medium for calling public attention to the relationship between animals and people. Reverence for animals was one of the themes in Joseph Beuys' work, *Coyote. I like America and America Likes Me*, which was performed in May 1974. For the artist, the endangered coyote symbolised the American West and the extermination of indigenous peoples who viewed the animal as sacred. To commemorate his first visit to the United States, Beuys lived with a coyote for a week, establishing a 'dialogue' with the animal. The performance consisted of ritualised movements in response to the animal's behaviour. In this work, the artist conjures up an ancient world where animal and human spirit intertwine.

Artists also used performance to address specific environmental problems. In 1969, Mierle Laderman Ukeles formulated her *Manifesto! Maintenance Art* (which was excerpted in *Artforum* in 1971) whose central idea was the 'perpetuation and maintenance of the species'. Beginning in 1977, Ukeles publicly promoted her ideas as Artist-in-Residence at the New York City Department of Sanitation. She executed some remarkable performances that heightened public awareness of the problems associated with urban waste. One of the highlights was *Touch Sanitation*, 1979-80, an 11-month performance that involved shaking the hands of every sanitation worker in New York City.

Ukeles' concern for educating the public about its role in stemming the tide of waste moved from the realm of performance to the creation of a permanent, indoor installation at the New York City Department of Sanitation's Marine Transfer Station. Titled *Flow City*, 1983-present, this work encompasses a passageway of recyclables, a 24-monitor media wall and a glass bridge for people to view the process of disposing urban waste.

While all forms of Environmental art help us to understand and renew our vital connection to the earth, ecological art offers creative solutions to environmental problems. Ecological art does not isolate and interpret aspects of nature but integrates them into a total network of relationships. The subject of each work becomes the land or cityscape and its inhabitants – the plants, animals, and human beings who live near or visit a site. This approach to art and nature is based on environmental ethics and the re-establishment of nature's equilibrium.

Ecological artists are social activists, weaving their ideas into the fabric of a community. Many stages in their long and complex art process depend upon collaboration with people from other fields – scientists, engineers, landscape architects. Some ecological artworks, like Patricia Johanson's *Leonhardt Lagoon*, actually revitalise natural and urban habitats, encouraging the optimal conditions for life. Others, like Helen and Newton Harrison's, *Breathing Space for the Sava River*, are more conceptual – creatively framing the problem, formulating an innovative plan and stimulating public participation in the environmental remediation effort.

The next challenge for ecological art is to find ways to preserve cultural diversity. In countries around the world, indigenous cultures are threatened as land becomes polluted or appropriated for development. Ecological art can address these problems by reinterpreting native rituals and traditions within the context of environmental problem solving. One way of cementing this interconnection between social and natural ecologies is to probe the roots of environmental ethics in non-Western societies. Collaboration with native artists is one way to accomplish this goal, resulting in a cross-fertilisation that ultimately enhances both Western and non-Western cultural traditions.

As countries strive to modernise their traditional foundations, it is essential to reclaim those beliefs which once fostered respect for the environment.

नागमा ठूलो गुण छ जसको मूल भोजन वायु हो । दूषित हावा मात्र आफूले भोजन गरी अस्वच्छ वायु अन्य प्राणीका लागि छोड्ने रीत भएकोले भगवान् शंकरका आभूषणमा नाग सर्प प्रधान भएको र नागजल रक्षक भगवान् वरुणका जल विभागका सदस्य पनि हुन् । यही कारणबाट नेपालमा नाग पञ्चमीको पर्व मनाउने सर्व विदितै कुरा हो ।

आजको काठमाडौं उपत्यकामा वायु र जल ज्यादै प्रदूषित भएकाले नागहरू हामीबाट टाढा हुँदै गएका छन् । हामीहरू नागपंचमी मनाएर र हाम्रो पर्यावरण स्वच्छ पारेर प्रकृति तथा हाम्रो परम्पराको सकारात्मक महत्त्वको कदर गरौं ।

Translated from Sanskrit, the poster reads: 'The naga deserves great respect because it breathes in polluted air and leaves fresh air for the survival of all living beings. This is why it is the main adornment of Lord Shiva. Nagas are also guardians of the waters and are part of the pantheon of god Varuna. These are the well known reasons why the Nag Panchami festival is celebrated in Nepal' (From Madan Mahon Mishra, Nepali Sanskritima Bagmati, 2047). The contemporary Nepali interpretation reads: 'In Kathmandu Valley today, the air and waters are so dirty that the nagas have deserted us. Let us respect nature and the positive values of our tradition by celebrating Nag Panchami and cleaning our environment.'

During a six-month sojourn in Nepal, I collaborated with Jyoti Duwadi, a Nepali-American artist, on an ecological artwork, *The Myth of the Nagas and the Kathmandu Valley Watershed*. We reinterpreted traditional art, myth and ritual within a contemporary environmental perspective, making them relevant and vital to a country in transition. What began as a ten-page position paper and plan of action was eventually translated into an exhibition in Kathmandu, sponsored by the Asian Development Bank to celebrate World Environment Day (in June 1993), organised by the United Nations Development Programme and the Nepali government.

This project addresses and offers solutions to the deteriorating environment in this once pristine Himalayan nation. By working with traditional artists, talking with scientists, public officials as well as a local environmental activists, we communicated ideas for a greenway and nature corridor along the rivers. The reclamation work, to be planted with native flora, would function as an ecological and cultural pilgrimage route as well as a buffer against the effects of sprawling urban growth.

Nepali mythology offers a wealth of environmental ethics and a means for communicating environmental remediation plans to the native people. Our artworks focused on the Nagas, serpent-deities and guardians of pure water, and the sacred forest of Kathmandu Valley where Shiva and other gods are believed to reside. While revitalising Kathmandu's unique cultural heritage, *The Myth of the Nagas* attempts to generate citizen interest and participation in the rehabilitation and maintenance of the riverine ecology.

One way of initiating projects like *The Myth of the Nagas* is through the auspices of the United Nations. Individual countries could sponsor Artist-in-Residency programmes. Artists from countries where ecological art has taken root can collaborate with and introduce the concept to native artists. Corporations, donor agencies, and non-government organisations abroad might also help underwrite an ecological artwork. With this type of sponsorship and institutional support, a truly international art movement with important ramifications for both culture and nature may result. As the United Nations approaches its 50th anniversary, an appropriate celebratory act could

include the support of artists working to protect culture and the environment.

The expensive Western aid and development projects, bequeathed to struggling nations worldwide, have mainly been technological in approach and often damaging to society and the environment. Ecological art offers an alternative approach to some of the problems confronting these countries. Ecological art helps to re-establish a sense of place and identity. Although technological solutions will also be necessary in some instances, it must be part of a total plan which integrates science and the arts. This more holistic approach to the planet's environmental and social problems represents a new pathway through the 21st century.

Nationally and regionally, an infrastructure is needed to achieve this vision. Ideally, sponsorship of artists working in communities should be the responsibility of federal and local governments, corporations, private foundations, and art and natural history museums.

Museums have an opportunity to redefine themselves and reshape the perceptions of their audience by supporting ecological art. Since the late 18th century, museums have mainly been repositories of objects for contemplation. In more recent times, they have weathered criticism for exhibiting art divorced from its context and for functioning at a distance from the public. Helping to sponsor ecological art gives museums the chance to play an activist role in the community.[4]

It is also important for leaders in all fields related to sustainable development to include artists in their team of consultants. From local master planning boards geared to urban and rural development to wide-ranging national initiatives and policy decisions, artists have a role to play both as advisors, planners and creators of artworks that rehabilitate the environment and reinvigorate the culture.

The crisis related to the rapid loss of nature and culture is a global issue. Therefore, their rejuvenation should be based on a synthesis of the environmental ethics of indigenous societies and the successful remediation efforts of industrialised nations. Through art, some of these ideas can be realised. As it has been for thousands of years before, art is a way to foster a harmonious relationship between people and nature.

Environmental Naga Panchami *Poster, 1993, conceived by Jyoti Duwadi and Barbara C Matilsky, painted by Deepak Joshi. In Nepal, small illustrations of the nagas are placed above the doorway of each home once a year to insure good fortune. On this day, called* Nag Panchami, *the serpent deities are worshipped. This poster was conceived as a prototype to be printed and distributed to the people of Kathmandu Valley. The Tanka-style painting interprets traditional* naga *illustrations from an environmental perspective showing the Kathmandu Valley as a lake, as described in the ancient text of the* Swayambhu Puran.

Notes

1 For an expanded discussion of this subject, see Barbara Matilsky, *Fragile Ecologies: Contemporary Artists' Interpretations and Solutions*, Rizzoli International, 1992.

2 Robert Hobbs, *Robert Smithson: Sculpture*, pp191-97.

3 As part of this exhibition, the museum selected Morris to execute an earthwork, *Johnson Pit #20*, at a

four-acre gravel quarry south of Seattle, Washington. The work has since sprouted a field of shrubs, trees and wildflowers, slowly camouflaging the geometric contouring of land designed by the artist.

4 See also: Barbara Matilsky, 'Art and Ecology: The Museum as Social Activist', *Museum News*, March – April 1992.

FROM ABOVE: The Social Mirror, *1983, Mierle Laderman Ukeles and city* *workers;* The Social Mirror, *1983, glass mirror on garbage truck, the truck* *is a permanent mobile public sculpture; Danehy Park, Cambridge, Mass,* *aerial view, photo Aronson*

MIERLE LADERMAN UKELES

RE-SPECT
An Interview by Amanda Crabtree

'*We have to change how we relate to the material world and artists are used to radically thinking things*'. Network Earth, CNN 28.2.93

'*Maintenance art is my attempt to get people to change the way they see maintenance workers and maintenance work as a whole, to appreciate the constant work and effort that maintenance work always involves*'. Network Earth, CNN 28.2.93

Mierle Laderman Ukeles has been creating public art events for the last 20 years to highlight what it is that keeps the city alive, the supposedly unheroic work that goes on in front of our very eyes without ever being seen. As artist-in-residence at the New York City Department of Sanitation, she intervenes within a larger notion of the environment through collaborations within the work situation, showing that it is possible to go beyond using the environmental crisis as a pretext to make art.

In 1969, Ukeles issued her *Manifesto! Maintenance Art*, a proposal to exhibit her daily household sweeping, cleaning, scrubbing as art. The city as home is a fundamental *leitmotif* which has developed in the work of Ukeles, who endeavours to show the interdependency of city life in her public art interventions. This was illustrated in 1979-80 by her first large-scale piece, *Touch Sanitation*, in which she shook the hand of every sanitation worker in the New York Sanitation Department and said to each individual 'Thank you for keeping New York City alive'.

In 1983, there was an art parade in New York City. Normally the Sanitation Department would have been there to tidy up after the event, but this time maintenance art went on display with *The Social Mirror*, which took the form of a mirrored garbage truck in the parade. *See Sanitation, See Yourself* was the original title of *The Social Mirror*, a very primitive mirror, which, as Mierle explains, 'catches you and puts you in the picture, you see yourself in the contents of the truck. I want people to simply see themselves inside the process of sanitation'.

And in order to let the public see – literally – the problem of waste recycling, Mierle Ukeles is constructing a mixed-media installation called *Flow City*, a public art environment at the Marine Transfer Station at 59th Street in mid-town Man-

hattan, New York. She intends to confront the public with the problem of waste disposal in an art work where visitors can actually penetrate the working environment. The piece is composed of three elements: a pedestrian ramp to the work area; a pedestrian corridor lined with panels of recycling materials – crushed glass, shredded rubber, batteries, newspapers; and a glass bridge entered from the pedestrian ramp where the spectator can observe trucks emptying their loads of rubbish onto waiting barges.

A wall of 24 video screens will bring sounds and images from the working surroundings in action, the recycling process, 'live' pictures of the Hudson river, and information about the wider ecological crisis emphasising maintenance work as an integral part of the natural functioning of the biosystem.

The cameras will also bring images from the Fresh Kills landfill on Staten Island, a borough on the outskirts of New York City. Fresh Kills, the largest man-made structure in the world, is a 3,000 acre site that has served as the dumping ground for New York's waste since the 1940s. Ukeles has been awarded a percent-for-art grant to develop a project for the landfill, another opportunity to bring the relationship between the city and its circulatory system into focus.

Another community landfill project is still in progress in Mayor Thomas W Danehy Park in Cambridge, Massachusetts. Mierle Ukeles has created four installations for this restored landfill, two of which have been completed. *Turnaround Surround* is a half-mile long glassphalt path incorporating recycled glass collected by the community and crushed and incorporated into the pathway; and *Smellers and Wavers*, aromatic and kinetic plants along the pathway which provide a multi sensory experience. Part three of the project will be five or six sculptural disc-shaped components for the top of the central mound formed of various recycled materials. Some discs will be flat to provide surfaces for skating or dancing and others will have relief elements for seating. The final part of the Danehy Park project involves 'putting richness back into the earth' through *Community Implants or Transplants*. Ukeles will collect donations of objects from the many different cultures represented in the Cambridge community, each item having significant memory value for the individual. The

Re-spect, *Givors, October 1993, FROM ABOVE: Mierle Laderman Ukeles discussing the project with the city workers; Children involved in the parade wearing adult work gloves; The parade of trucks down to the river*

Photos Herve Hugues and Jacques Del Pino

object, accompanied by a short statement by the donor describing its importance, will be placed in a container to be implanted in the discs.

Memory, individual and collective, is an inherent aspect of many of Mierle Ukeles' projects, and was particularly apparent in her urban performance *Re-spect*, at Givors in October 1993. Givors is a small French town, on the banks of the Rhône, 20 kilometres south of Lyons, where in 1749, a royal glassworks was established. The glass factory still exists and is one of the last surviving industries in a town marked by a current history of disindustrialisation and unemployment. The piece succeeded in uniting the past and present of the town in a most spectacular way, whilst also emphasising the great natural force and presence of the Rhône.

In 1993, Ukeles was invited to participate in a public art project in Givors initiated by the Institut pour l'Art et la Ville, an institution directed by Alain Charre and Jacky Vieux, which has been researching public commissions and alternative practice for the last five years. The experimental programme 'L'Art, la Ville et la Route' was devised in relation to the on-going municipal urban redevelopment of the Route Nationale 86, a main road which crosses Givors. Five artists and a landscape designer were invited to participate in a debate on the relevance of art within the context of urban redevelopment.

Ukeles' proposal consisted of a collaboration with city workers, gardeners, dustmen, firemen and river authority personnel with whom she worked very closely. An assortment of 30 city vehicles, various sports associations and children on bicycles or wearing used work gloves were led by the city band in an unorthodox celebratory parade down the Route Nationale 86 to the banks of the Rhône. The different vehicles then proceeded to perform a 'ballet mécanique' on the quayside of the river, with movements such as the 'snake' or the 'spider' devised by the drivers and coordinated by the artist. This was paralleled simultaneously on the river by a choreography with rowing boats, rescue speedboats, barges and a tow boat. Gradually a 100 ton diamond of re-cycled cobalt blue glass from the local glass factory was revealed, recalling the town's historic links with glass.

By inviting the public to look again at the daily life of the city, this urban performance became a spectacular event which paid tribute to ordinary social practice, proving that creative and productive alternatives are possible. Mierle Laderman Ukeles demonstrates that large-scale land projects can assume a genuine public dimension, heightening public awareness of modern society's relationship to larger ecological systems

Mierle Laderman Ukeles Thinking about this interview is hard for me, because I ended up having a huge emotional response to the whole thing, much more than I had expected. I think it's going to end up being one of the rare moments of my whole life because so many things came together. I mean none of us knew really what was going to happen, trucks could have fallen off into the water, they could have crashed into each other, people could have got run over, we could have had another flood. So many things could have gone wrong and they didn't, and this thing came together in such a magical way. People ask how much was the budget, like half a million dollars? I laugh and they say how long was it? And I say an hour and they laugh again because I make it sound like it took weeks or something!

Amanda Crabtree *The title of your piece was 're-spect' and not respect, what is the significance of the hyphen?*
The hyphen is meaningful to me, because re-hyphen-spect really means to look again. We are talking about an ancient material, an ancient town, an ancient means of transportation, very old fashioned work, the issue of people who do very necessary work and whether they get respect. At a meeting with the city workers, I said 'do you feel that your work is honoured?' and they were very strong in saying no. I heard the same old thing, people don't respect us, they don't think we do anything, and then the one worker said to me, 'so what you're going to do, is that going to get us any respect?' and I said to him, 'I don't know if what I'm going to do is going to do anything!'

He questioned me in a hard, almost aggressive way, as if he had expectations in his question. He put me on the line and this piece was initiated right there, from that one person. These are people who remove waste so the city doesn't get sick and I felt that the man was saying a lot of things, there was tremendous compression in his question: 'I'm stuck with reality – do you really have anything to say to me or is it just a fantasy?'

From then on, I knew I was on solid ground, that we had a way to communicate. I knew that he would be watching me, to see if I was really serious, as serious as he. In fact, he did watch me with enormous intensity throughout the whole performance work, and I watched him too and the work spoke to him, it moved him. I don't know what the work accomplished in a lot of ways but I know that it hit a lot of people and I felt we were creating a valid piece of culture there that day.

– And so how does that man and his role in the city link up with your notion of how the city functions?
I think that this notion of re-spect was in the hyphen. The project gave the workers an opportunity to step outside their own shoes and look again, see themselves from a different vantage point. I watched the workers watching each other

and the city people watch them. There was all this seeing again, layers of seeing upon seeing, which is also what culture does, a mirroring back of certain conditions. So they saw how beautifully they work first of all, how much they fit the land next to the river. Complex things became visible in a very clear way.

Their choreography was not the most complicated in the world but it was very beautiful. They worked with each other like they know how to do very well but they also worked in the place and performed in front of the people, which is what their work really consists of anyhow. They were able to encapsulate what they do stretched out over years and years into this one occasion.

– Did the people look at them differently?
I think so. I think there was a kind of looking though layers. The fact of the children being part of it was another 're'. They were the main human element of the procession through the town, linked to the work by wearing those big adult work gloves. They were seen anew I think and they could also see themselves as hooked into all this. I hoped they would see that the town is a place for them and that the other people would see the children as in their place, which is the whole town not locked up in their housing estate, and that there was a place for everybody.

– What about the river? You were asked to work on an idea of the Route Nationale 86 and you linked it with the river – what was behind that?
Well, any notion of the environment, any ecological notion immediately needs to link up the land and the water. We literally came out of water but we are land creatures. It's that simple. I have a strong feeling that rivers are the life element of the town and in Givors you have this magnificent river. How could one not want to come to the river even though many of us have turned our backs on the river in cities?

The river used to be the way for work, transportation, communication, the way of connection, just like the Route Nationale was. I wanted us to have a new view of both of them – both are paths that feed each other or should feed each other. So the critical thing about the RN 86 and the river is that they are both paths, you can work on them and celebrate on them, there's a certain fluidity in both of them. I wanted to bring them together, to bring a flow from one end to another. The feeding between the land and water needs to be much more flowing than it is. A lady said to me 'you've returned the river to us tonight' and I felt that.

– The performance nearly had to be cancelled because the Rhône was so high and the quayside was flooded. How did you deal with this powerful force that we were trying to work with?
I remember someone saying I don't know if you'll be able to do this and that movement because the river's moving so fast. In other words we were picking up on the river in its scary manifestations; nature in this 'bigger than us' aspect. This is very good for us to reckon with, it's a very good scale-establisher.

There was also the meeting with Bernard, the captain of the barge, with his son and the other ponton captains. We got to see this lovely little slither of a life that actually comes from a very long, very ancient tradition . . . kind of rare today.

Anyhow, this incredible cobalt blue diamond, this fabulous sight was delivered by people who are very calm and competent and at ease in the environment. It was sort of dangerous, messing around trying to do certain patterns where the water was flowing so hard; there was a kind of risk that they were willing to be involved in. Those people pushed to the limit, which meant they were taking this thing as far as they could take it and they were saying to me that they really cared about this thing.

And at the end, when the fire-fighters were climbing up in the dark and you couldn't really see them and that 75 metre ladder truck was going up to the moon, the other fire-fighter was feeding water to the water, it was so absurd. They looked like space-age creatures, and they were holding this technological hose, they were sort of recycling water to the water but in a very ritualistic manner. It was this notion of return, of power, of energy that would come back to us and the river can give that sense to us.

– And what about the blue glass?
I thought of the blue glass in terms of Royal Blue and the reason I thought of that is that the most viable industry left in Givors is the VMC glassworks which has been going on since the 18th century. The French have been involved in blue for a very long time, from royalty all the way down to Yves Klein who also knew about the magical power of blue.

The reason the blue was in a diamond shape was to give it a sign of value even though it was really garbage that was thrown out, crushed, this rather degraded material, having lost its form and getting ready to go back into the oven for another turn. But this diamond shape was declaring it had value, it was a new look at this material which is a very long-term interest of mine.

The people who invited me to do this were willing to go to such huge lengths to get this material, and then build this crib to hold it and transport it. I mean none of these things were there, everything had to be created. We had to get the people to donate the glass, get the glass transported by means that aren't usually used to transport this kind of material, find a place to unload the glass, and also to load the glass, find the barges etc. Everything crossed boundaries:

'Ballet méchanique' with the trucks on the quayside of the River Rhône

FROM ABOVE: Choreography with rowing boats, rescue speed-boats, barges and a tow boat on the river gradually reveals a 100 ton diamond of re-cycled cobalt blue glass; One of the firefighters 'feeding water to the water' provides a grand finale

different kinds of industry, different ways of working, different kinds of people. A whole new ecology was created based on moving this recycleable material deeper into society. This just proved what can be done, which is exactly how we need to create millions of new connections to have a more healthy relationship to the planet. That's a bigger picture, but it was proved that it is possible, that you can have power in the world to do these things.

– What about you in all this? I mean, in many ways, Givors could not be more different than New York and yet you seemed to be very much at home.
Which was rather strange, don't you think? I ask myself that also. Now I came to Givors very much with this intellectual idea about the place. I was very much informed by the concept of the megalopolis, where relationships among places and among cultures even inside of one place have become so complex and jagged that a little town doesn't necessarily mean a little town and a big town necessarily mean a big town anymore. There's a scale issue that transcends size and these jagged shifts happen because of electronic networks and because of technology and travelling across space and time electronically. We're changed creatures, I think, and yet very much tied to the earth because we are earthlings, so there's this enormous contradictory thing going on within us as social creatures. I also have had a lot of experience working with city workers who do the universal work of keeping a city alive. I could go anywhere and I would know a lot of things about a lot of these workers.

Now, what was stupefying about Givors was that the size of the town worked very much in our favour. The response to the work that we did was vast and I would say that we had 80 per cent of the city's trucks in our piece. What was magical was that the involvement and the connections that were necessary to make this piece happen were working at an immense scale. I was very mindful of that and very grateful to have most of the vehicles of the city, most of the representatives of the different kinds of workers of the city and representatives of regional and national bodies. All this made it possible for us to do all the different things that we did compressed in that one time. The size of the city only made the frame more perceptible, huge effort, huge involvement within a manageable size, so you could get the awesomeness of the scale in a manageable

experience and I don't know if that will ever happen to me again in my whole life.

To accomplish that level of response in New York I think you would have to put the whole city up in aeroplanes just to be able to look down to see so much of the city in one place at one time. It was an ability to see the wholeness which I think was the finest thing about it. In terms of any environmental or ecological lust, it was fulfilled in the wholeness of what happened, in the wholeness of response, in so many people pushing this idea to the maximum. That's where me with my big New York eyes was so satisfied in Givors.

– So what role can the artist hope to play in all this?
First of all, it's incredible to me that this thing happened. I feel like I threw a ball into the air and many people played with it. It was a true public art work in that it was born in public, it wasn't one artist doing a work alone in a studio. This was a vision that was realised in public which is something else and it tapped into a power, a kind of democratic power. I think that people felt there was a kind of truth, that this could really happen in reality, that it wasn't just a sentence written down like a wish but it really did happen.

That guy in the forklift truck did a ballet, he was as graceful as any ballet dancer ever and the cherry pickers kissed, they really did kiss and the diamond was born on the water and we were able to get across the language barrier and create something together. What's important about this is that the world is in need of huge creative risk taking, of doing things in different ways and doing them together. We really need to do a lot of things like that because there are a lot of things wrong in the world. Now what this one hour showed was that there is power in each of us to do that, we can affect the world, we *can* make things happen that did not exist before in that way. That's when the workers looked at each other and said, we do a lot of things, the children said we belong to an amazing town and the people looked at the children who saw themselves locked into the town and not separated, and this material was returned as beauty. All that was abundantly clear.

This was an artist's vision that was realised in public. That's what can happen. And what I also liked so much was that there was so much respect handed back to me, to an unbelievable level. My vision was respected, my idea, my ideal was respected, so enormously, that's what makes it so hard to talk about.

WOLFGANG LAIB

BEYOND THE IMAGINATION
An Interview by Clare Farrow

Wolfgang Laib was born on 25 March 1950, in Metzingen, Germany. He studied medicine at the University of Tubingen and became a doctor in 1974, though he chose not to practise. In 1975 he made the first milkstone and two years later he collected pollen for the first time. He began to use rice in 1983 and beeswax in 1987. Working alone with these organic materials – sifting the pollen, pouring the milk, sanding and polishing the stone, melting and building with the beeswax – Laib has produced works that turn the imagination upside down. Small becomes big, ordinary becomes extraordinary, lightness balances weight, and the end becomes also the beginning. The work is seductive and spellbinding, but it is also chaste and pure. The pollen is fragile and volatile, and yet this powder that can be sifted through the finest muslin has the potential to create a vast forest. The milk evaporates in the air, and yet its energy and lightness can reduce the weight of the marble on which it rests in perfect equilibrium. There is a reality, Laib argues, that is beyond the imagination. It seems magical, but it is there, just in front of you.

Since 1976 Laib has shown his work in cities around the world, from New York and Chicago, to Paris, London, Stuttgart and Tokyo, and has recently had solo exhibitions at The Museum of Contemporary Art in Los Angeles, the Kunstmuseum Bonn, and the capc Musée d'art contemporain, Bordeaux. He is represented by Sperone Westwater in New York, and continues to live and work in a small village in southern Germany. The following interview was recorded in London on 24 October 1993.

Clare Farrow *You work in tune with the rhythm of the seasons. Can you talk about this with reference to the process of collecting pollen from the dandelions, buttercups, pines, etc, that flower in the fields and forests close to your studio?*

Wolfgang Laib I collect the pollen from the flowers, bushes and trees near the village where I live. The process begins in early spring with the hazelnut and continues with the dandelion, buttercup and pine. It is a period of four or five months. After this I have four or five jars of pollen. I collect the pollen with my hands, shaking it into a small jar. It's very simple.

– It must be very delicate, careful work.
It's not really about care. I think it's something different. It goes beyond that, which is what makes it so important for me.

– How close do you come, when collecting the pollen, to feeling part of the creative cycle of generation, development, flowering, and decay?
Working with this, you become not just a part of it but the same. You feel very close to it. I'm the only one who collects the pollen, but I try to involve other people too, in pouring the milk onto the stone, in sifting the pollen. For me, having this experience with things, in your daily life and work, brings you into a completely different world, in your own life. From the outside the work seems repetitive, but when you are doing it, it doesn't seem so. You don't even realise it's repetitive. It's just, that's what it is. It's like day and night. Next morning, the sun will rise again but you don't think of it as a repetition.

– When you are collecting the pollen, do you concentrate your thoughts on the act itself?
Most probably it is what other people would call meditation. If you concentrate on something enough, you reach the point where you are no longer conscious of your own concentration. I think that is the state I am longing for.

– So does the process of collecting the pollen bring about a feeling of calm, and equilibrium?
Yes, I think so. It's not so easy to put these things into words, you know.

– When it's warm and the sun shines you can collect a lot of pollen. When it's cold and windy you can collect only a little. Four or five months of this labour produce only four or five jars containing three or four different types of pollen. The process seems on the outside to involve an unreasonable amount of effort and time, considering how little is visibly gained. You seem to be challenging this notion, that one must justify one's actions purely in terms of the material gain.
I feel just the opposite to what most people do. This work is concerned with something totally different in terms of your whole meaning, what you think you have to do with your life, what you gain and what you don't gain, what is big and what is small, what is much and what is little – all

OPPOSITE: Wolfgang Laib in the buttercup meadow

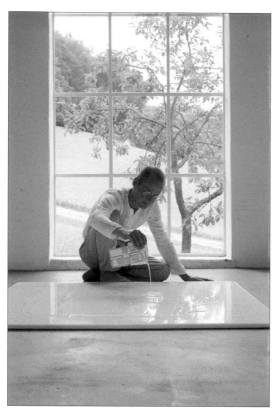

these things become the opposite of what we are used to, and it becomes a question of everything and all. There is something other than what we see and think we achieve.

– You accept what is there, for the short time that it is there, and you make use of it. You have only a little of the dandelion and buttercup pollen because there is only a little. You have more of the pine pollen because there is more. The dandelion pollen is orange-gold, the pine pollen a lighter yellow. You have not chosen the colours of these organic substances. It's like the blue of the sky or the whiteness of milk.
Certainly, the milk is what it is. It's not just a white liquid or a white paint. I could not create the milk, and that is the chance, that is what is beautiful and important. It's not something I could paint or sculpt. The pollen is not a yellow pigment which I have made a painting with. There is much, much more than myself, than I could ever make myself.

– You are the only one to collect the pollen. Why do you prefer to work in solitude?
When I am working it's very important for me to be alone. I live in a very small village. Being alone I feel independent and can work out of this solitude and create my own work. I'm travelling a lot now, but still I spend months and months by myself. I'm always going back because that is where my work comes from.

– You have spoken about hermits and ascetics living in forests and mountain caves, saying that one can achieve more through renunciation. Can you comment on this?
Yes, that's exactly what I think, that in renouncing you achieve much more. I have had a dream for a long time now to create one of my beeswax spaces in a mountain cave, and I hope this will soon take shape and become a reality. I spent a month in France recently, in the Pyrénées, and I want to do the work there. I hope it will be soon.

– It's a wonderful thought. Such a work will seem to have been concealed within the mountain for a very long time, I imagine.
Yes, it is a work about this . . . When I talk about renouncing, I am talking about it in the widest sense imaginable.

– You have also spoken about St Francis preaching to the birds. Is it only in solitude, do you think, that one can communicate with nature?
I can only speak for myself. But yes, I think so.

– You store the pollen in jars. How do you conserve the colour?
The colour is amazingly consistent. I have had pollen for 15 years and the colour has not changed. There is a difference, however, be-

tween the types of pollen. For instance, dandelion pollen is very coarse and organic, so you have to be very careful with it. Actually, when dandelion pollen changes it's not that it's losing its colour in the way that colour is affected by daylight, for example, it's more that it dries up like a flower petal and it doesn't have its fresh colour any more. But it's not like a pigment, it's an organic material that dries. The pine pollen is very fine, like dry sand, and you would have to throw water on it to destroy it. Humidity and cold are not good for it at all. I keep the pollen in very simple jars and open the jars when I like, and close them when I like. I have not been very careful about conservation. I realise that when the works go to other places, the questions of conservation come up. But it's not something that interests me.

– What is most important to you about the pollen? Is it the colour that seems to hover with the intensity of sunlight; or the concentration of vital energy contained in only a tiny cone of the fragile substance; or is it the purity of the sifted material which is so light and volatile?
The important thing is what the pollen is. It is all the things you have said but maybe it is also many more things, things that maybe I don't know and you don't know. I am very disappointed if people see it only as a visual, aesthetic experience. The pollen does have an incredible colour, but it is not a painting and it is far away from Klein, or Rothko.

– In your work the pollen becomes visible as an organic substance that is both ordinary and extraordinary, powerful and vulnerable, a material which is not respected or valued as it should be.
Yes. I have been amazed to meet people whose only connection to the pollen is hay fever! They have nothing else to say. They have no connection to the simplest things. They are so far away from seeing these important things. The more the situation is like that, the more I feel it is important to do this work, to try to change this situation.

– Is there an ecological argument in the work?
Of course that is there somewhere. My work questions the whole situation in this society, and in one sense it is very political. But that's not enough for me. Society is aware of the ecological argument, you don't need an artist to say it. The discussion in our society is more about repairing things. I want a total change. I don't just want to gain more through repairs.

– Is it important, do you think, for an artist to remain at a distance from politics?
Yes. I think it's very important for an artist to be free. You can do much, much more if you are free.

And you can always be true to yourself.
This is why I became an artist and not a politician.

– *Can you describe how you sift the pollen?*
It's something very beautiful, something very simple that I like very much. I sift the pollen through very fine muslin. It has to be a different fineness for the different pollens because some are coarse and some are fine. That's all. Just sifting the pollen, squatting on the floor. The most beautiful thing is that I can start and do it for as long as I want. The time it takes depends very much on the pollen. For instance, I have only a small jar of the dandelion pollen, which is not full. It is very coarse and organic, and it sifts very slowly, and a piece on the floor would be something like 60 x 80cm. It will take me some hours to do this small dandelion piece. On the other hand, I have four jars of the pine pollen, collected over two seasons. They are very big jars, full of very fine pollen. It sifts very, very quickly; it comes out like clouds. So at the same time as I have a small dandelion piece, I have a huge pine pollen piece, say 400 x 500cm. For my first exhibitions I sifted the pollen onto glass because the galleries often had floors that were wooden and cracked and at that time I could not ask them to change the floors. But now I do. The floor has to be good enough for me to sift the pollen directly onto it. When the exhibition ends, I re-sift the pollen through muslin, to separate it from the dust that has collected, so the pollen can be used again.

– *You have talked about the 'colouful miracle' of the dandelion pollen, about its 'energies and powers'. Do you see it as a magical substance?*
It might seem magical to you, but I think it is not. It is the same with the milk and the pollen. I have poured the milk and sifted the pollen so often, but the experience always remains new. It's something you have never seen before, a reality which you cannot believe is a reality. It seems impossible, but then it is there, just in front of you.

– *Why did you become dissatisfied with medicine? You have said that art can have a visionary power. Can it also have a healing power?*
Yes, certainly. For me, the most difficult thing about studying medicine was that it is a natural science which follows only logic. It sees the body as a material body. Our whole culture is based on such thinking. It seems so successful and yet it is so limited, limited to the material world. The more I studied, the more I heard what I was taught, the more over-sensitive I became about all this. I just couldn't believe what I was taught. I just couldn't believe that this was all there was. I think it is a part, but then there is much more. These bodies I saw in the hospitals were human beings. So I began to search for something else – for another body. It was shocking for me to see doctors knowing everything about the material body, knowing and being able to do things which mankind could never do before, but then knowing nothing about what goes beyond that, and, in many cases, being more primitive than ever.

– *Can you talk about your interest in India?*
Since my childhood I have been quite often in Asian countries, not only India. Certainly that has been a very important influence, but from the outside there have been a lot of misunderstandings. This morning I visited the Victoria & Albert Museum – I wanted to see the exhibition of Russian icons – and I walked through some of the rooms with European art and remnants of European life from the last few centuries. It is almost unbelievable, this idea of culture, of what is important and what is not. It is a relief to look at something Egyptian or African, Asian or prehistoric, or from the Christian Middle Ages. Over the years, I have become more and more disgusted with European culture since the Renaissance, including its predecessors in Roman and Greek culture. And my experience with natural science, which comes out of the ideas of the Renaissance, led me to search for something totally different. It is now 500 years after the Renaissance and I believe it is time for a change, for a complete change in our thinking, in what we do, think and feel, in what we find important and not important. It's not the time to add another invention or another painting, but to search for something completely different. This is why I am interested in other cultures which are independent from our own, from the Roman and the Greek, cultures which can show us things which we never knew, which are so revolutionary for life today, and for life in the future – things which challenge everything we know or are used to. I am very interested in religions like Islam or Buddhism and Jainism, or in the Franciscans, but that is not to say that I would ever become a Sufi or a Buddhist or a Franciscan. That would be the opposite of what I want. I could never be so close to something historical. I am interested in the present and the future, in trying to find something else for our life and for the future.

– *You sometimes heap the pollen into small cones, like tiny mountains, directly onto the floor or onto brass plates from India. You have described these cones of pollen as being 'so precious, so fragile, so small and yet so big . . . '*
The work you are talking about is *The Five Mountains Not To Climb On*. They are five mountains of buttercup pollen, only 7cm high. I think it is one of my major works, one that gives a sense of what I have been doing, what I think about things.

– *You have also heaped rice onto these brass plates which are used in India to bring food and flowers into the temple . . .*
Yes, but also they are very simple plates that people use in daily life. I also use these plates

because they are very abstract in shape. I chose to use rice because it is an essential food. I could have used wheat, but I chose rice because it is more abstract, and it is white.

– Do simplicity, repetition, and purity enter into your daily life as well as your work?
I have always tried to have a very simple life. Change has to begin in your daily life, it is there that the revolution begins, and out of there your work has to come. So I hope my work and my life have become one. Simplicity leads you to renounce, to an ascesis. I am not searching for a formal simplicity, like the minimalists. I ask much more. Acts which, on the outside, seem like rituals and a search for purity, on the inside seem the most normal of all. How else would you do something or treat something?

– Can you talk about your notion of beauty?
I am not afraid of beauty, unlike most artists today. The pollen, the milk, the beeswax, they have a beauty that is incredible, that is beyond the imagination, something which you cannot believe is a reality – and it is the most real. The beauty is there and you have to be ready for it. I could not make it myself, I could not create it myself, but I can participate in it. Trying to create it yourself is only a tragedy, participating in it is a big chance.

– Your work is both chaste and sensual. Milk is an organic substance that suggests intimacy and vitality. It is also white, the colour of purity. Is this how you see it?
Yes. It is amazing when chaste and sensual become very close or even the same.

– How important is the simple gesture of pouring the milk onto the marble?
You might call it a ritual and most probably it is a ritual, but for me it is a very simple act – pouring milk on a stone. In doing this – and not only myself, it is important for me that other people become involved – you become very close to the two elements which are so different and eventually become one. It is such a simple gesture that it becomes a challenge for most of us.

– The white milk on white stone calls to mind the paintings of Malevich, and also Robert Ryman. Do you feel an affinity with either of these artists?
Well, my father was very interested in Malevich and I grew up with a lot of influence from Malevich. I lived in this very small village in southern Germany. There was a small town nearby where around 50 Malevich paintings were stored until 1958 when they were sold to the Stedelijk in Amsterdam. My father was close to an artist there, and the paintings were with an architect there. They were all rolled up and under

a bed. I never saw them then. I was too small. But my father was very interested. There was an exhibition of the paintings before they left and I have seen a photograph of myself when I was eight years old, standing in front of a painting by Malevich, a yellow rectangle. (laughter)
I'm a close friend of Robert Ryman, but I have to say that a Ryman painting and a milkstone are very different. And I think Bob Ryman knows that too. Milk is not a white liquid, and pollen is not a yellow pigment.

– The milk that is poured on the marble becomes so still, so at one with the stone, that for the few hours in which this equilibrium is maintained, the milkstone seems timeless.
Yes. It is something that is beyond time limits.

– This period of stillness, of the milk coming to rest on the marble, this balancing of weight and lightness, why do you find it so beautiful?
Why? I cannot explain. It is something so unbelievable this reality. It's so far beyond the imagination. It is absolutely still, the milk, this liquid, that would normally flow away.

– You have described the stone as 'a being like the milk'. What did you mean by this?
Stone is a living being – like milk, pollen, animals, human beings, or mountains. Other cultures have seen stone in this way and you find these ideas all over the world, and also thousands of years ago. Only for us did it become something we would not believe, because we separated ourselves from all of that.

– How did you decide on the shape of the milkstones?
For me it was like a detail of something bigger. One milkstone is then one object and I've made many milkstones, big ones and small ones. I searched for something very abstract and still. Of course you could say that the circle is the perfect still shape, but for me, with the two eyes, I thought that the rectangle – close to the square – was the least distracting shape.

– How important is space to you? I'm thinking of your words 'where emptiness is fullness'. This seems to be in keeping with your belief in simplicity and purity; also the notion that something small can also be big. Do you believe that space is beautiful in itself, not an emptiness to be filled?
Yes. First, it is the space in which you live and work; and second, it is the public space in which you exhibit your works. I like spaces which are very empty, not full of clutter; just a simple place to be. That is also the reason why I do not like furniture, because it somehow occupies and destroys every space. My life is on the floor, not on tables and chairs. I sleep on the floor, I sit and

eat on the floor, and my work is on the floor. People speak about floor sculpture, but it is much more than that, it is not about pedestals or no pedestals. Since my childhood, I have seen spaces in Asian countries, big empty spaces in mosques, small huts or houses, just an empty room with some pillows or mats – what a relief from all this clutter which we seem to need in Europe. Empty space is totally unknown in our culture and yet it seems the most normal thing.

– What would your ideal exhibition space be like?
I could not say that there would be one ideal space. But what I just said about spaces to live and work in, I would also ask, or I would like to ask of spaces to show art in public: a simple space with beautiful light, a beautiful floor and white walls. But the reality is very different with all the museums which have been built recently around the world. It is very disappointing for me and the opposite of what I would need or what other artists would like to have. Artists and curators have searched for alternatives in old warehouses or factories and they are mostly very good for showing art. But then it is very dissatisfying that it seems impossible to build a new space now for art. For myself, I find the big space in the museum in Bordeaux one of the most beautiful spaces to exhibit in. It is a warehouse built in the last century and it almost looks like a cathedral, but somehow it is not a museum, and it is not a church. The space has, I think, a spirituality which other spaces do not have. And it would be very beautiful and necessary to achieve something like this in a contemporary building. Of course not every museum would have to look like Bordeaux. A diversity in exhibition spaces is very good and important. We need more extraordinary situations like Bordeaux, but they just do not exist.

– Do you like the idea of exhibition spaces being away from cities?
Sometimes, but not always. Sometimes, it can be a very beautiful situation, up to the extreme which I have explained to you.

– The mountain cave . . .
Yes. But then, on the other hand, especially for me, living in a small village and doing my work, it is sometimes very important to make an exhibition for many people, and then it has to be in one of the big cities. It's very beautiful to make something in a very isolated village and then to show it somewhere like New York.

– Working with beeswax, you have made passages and small houses. The houses cannot be entered. The passages do not go anywhere. Can you explain why?
I had an exhibition in Bordeaux which was called *Passage*. There was one arch which was really

closed with beeswax. It was closed and it was called *Passage*. It was something that was closed but it was also something to enter into another world. Seeing the Russian icons today was very beautiful for me, because they are about this. For me, empty and full can be reversed, and can even be the same.

– The beeswax is scented, the colour is golden. Why did you choose to work with this material? Was it a simple step from working with the pollen?
I thought about it for a long time before I made the first piece. It's very close to pollen. It's a material that I did not make. It's the building material of the bees. When you have a piece of beeswax next to a table or a chair, it's another world. It's like there are worlds in between.

– Are the black openings in the beeswax passages again to do with the notion that an ending can become, in a sense, a beginning?
The beeswax passages which end in a black opening, it's like something beyond, into another world.

– There is an equilibrium in your working process, a balancing of activities, in the sense that you collect the pollen every time the flowers are in bloom, you sand and polish the marble for the milkstones, and melt and build with the beeswax when you have the materials and the time to do so. One activity does not banish the others.
Yes. For me, it's not like then and then and then. It's like doing it again.

Your work seems to be about accepting things as they are, about participating in a creative process that is more inventive and extraordinary than the artist's imagination, about working with substances that have energies and powers that we may not even fully comprehend. Can you talk about your notion of time and the individual?
I think the idea of the individual in our culture is a misunderstanding that leads to the tragedy which every individual is in. Other cultures have seen the individual as part of everything and they did not have this tragedy. From the beginning, I thought this work ought to be anonymous, rather than the work of Wolfgang Laib. It goes beyond the individual. But this was the only way in which I could bring the work into the world, and show what I think about these things. If you believe only in the individual, in what you are, then life is a tragedy that ends in death. But if you feel part of a whole, that what you are doing is not just you, the individual, but something bigger, then all these problems are not there any more. Everything is totally different. There is no beginning and no ending.

FROM ABOVE: Passage, 1992, beeswax, wood construction, 790 x 522cm, Installation at the capc Musée d'art contemporain, Bordeaux; Pollen from Hazelnut, 1986, 320 x 360cm, installation at capc Musée d'art contemporain, Bordeaux

INTRODUCTION TO TICKON

GERTRUD KØBKE SUTTON

In 1970 a Sicilian, Alfio Bonanno, settled in Denmark on the island of Langeland. He was an artist and arrived without prejudice or preconceived ideas. He soon made his mark as an artist working in many different media and was one of the first to create sculptures composed of boulders and tree trunks in the landscape.

Since the early 80s, Bonanno has dreamt of a total amalgam of art and nature. In a project from 1983 he describes how he imagines a landscape with 'structures' of materials found on the spot. Some of the constructions would be situated like islands in marshes and lakes and be inaccessible, while others should be able to withstand the use of human beings and animals. What was man-made would become part of the cycle in nature and transformed by decomposition. The place should truthfully illustrate the transformation and cycles of all living things. The realisation of this dream did not offer itself until 1990.

Having lived on the island for some 20 years, Bonanno has a great feeling of solidarity with the place, its nature and the people living there, and it was a *sine qua non* that, if realised, his project was to be situated in Langeland.

Langeland is a long and narrow island placed between Funen and Sealand. The soil is fertile and the landscape undulating farm and woodland, richly endowed with archaeological sites, medieval churches and country houses. During the last five years there has, however, been a drastic change in living conditions on the island. Public expenditure has been cut, unemployment has increased and social services reduced, schools and hospitals have suffered and many small enterprises have had to close down. The human reactions have been negative, unsettling and with a marked lack of initiative. For Bonanno this situation called for action and his profound attachment to the idea of an existentialist and international project in the environment of Langeland must be seen in this context.

Having for some time advocated the creation of a centre for art in nature, in 1990, he was approached by the county council of Tranekær. This was followed by an offer of 60 acres for the free disposal of the centre by Count Ahlefeldt-Laurvig of Tranekær Castle. A committee was formed with the Count, Tranekær City Council, art historians and critics, a writer and the Director of the Kunsthallen Brandts, Odense. An old building next to the castle was secured as a guest house and workshop for the artists.

Had it not been for Alfio Bonanno's enthusiasm and his talent for making the locals participate and support the project politically and socially, it would all have been in vain. With their knowledge of the landscape, traditions, history and handicrafts of the island, they are now partners in the initiative.

For three years Bonanno has devoted his life to TICKON (*Tranekær Internationale Center for Kunst og Natur*) and his activities as a sculptor and painter have had to come second. In the beginning this caused him some frustration, yet little by little he realised that for the time being TICKON was his work.

He organised meetings with schools, local industries, the three city councils on the island and the county council of Funen. He lectured at home and abroad and contacted a worldwide range of artists. With the support and collaboration of city and county councils as well as state and private funds the first artists were invited in 1991.

Since the 1970s there has been a change in attitude and an increased feeling of responsibility among artists working in, and with, nature. TICKON is to be a testing ground for art and for ideas that may enhance the enjoyment of nature. We hope to encourage sculptors, composers or poets to create the unexpected and to turn ecological issues into aesthetic ones. And by creating encounters and collaboration between artists and specialists in all fields, from farmers and artisans to biologists, zoologists,

botanists, etc, it is hoped to foster creativity and a more enhanced understanding of the mechanisms of a specific locality and of the frailty and resilience of its nature.

Tranekær Castle and village is the natural focal point for Langeland. The castle grounds with its old and rare trees, a lake and fields, meadows and woods are at the disposal of TICKON. Here the artists have worked – 14 to date – and more are to come. Each one has chosen his or her special place within the area and proposed a plan of action. The necessary materials have been provided and helpers, machinery and so on arranged according to their needs. Some work with trees, some build with twigs and plants that may grow or wither, some use stones, bones, leaves or just words and the sound of the wind. The intervention may be totally ephemeral, only to survive in a photograph. The dialogue and symbiosis between art and nature has first priority.

Different stages of the artists' work have been registered in photos and video as a basis for publications and many of them have presented us with models, drawings and texts. To this must be added the important materials sent from the ever-growing network of related activities all over the world. With new artists arriving every year, the presentation of this material will be an important part of the activities of TICKON. It is our plan to seek the help of international architects in a competition for an inspired and unconventional building for the collection.

Alfio Bonanno, FROM ABOVE, L TO R: Different works constructed to be used by Teatro Stabile di Bergamo (open air theatre/performance) for 'Culture without Borders', Holstebro, Denmark, September 1993, in collaboration with Odin Theatre and Teatro Stabile di Bergamo, Italy

Alfio Bonanno, LEFT: Fossil Snail, 1992, Krakamarken, Denmark, main work and details of stone entrance (approx 15.5m diameter), photo (above) Jørn Ronnau; OPPOSITE: Built for the duration of 24 hours on the site where the straw was harvested, Holeby, Denmark, 1991

JANE BALSGAARD
LAVENDER PASSAGE

My thoughts about sculpture tend to be directed towards the sky. I am drawn towards that which is light and floating. Fascinated by the idea of renouncing gravity, my imagination plays with sculptures that are transparent and soaring into space, objects liberated from terrestrial ties. However, the Tranekær ground gave me quite a different impulse. The ancient farmland spotted with Stone Age burial mounds called for close contact with the earth and the soil, where flint axes and gold tankards may be hidden. At such a place it is important to work in collaboration with the cycles of nature. A lump of earth split in two with the scent of lavender, opening like a hill of trolls. Fundamentally the shape is geometrical but in time it will decay and the ivy-covered exterior will weigh it to the ground, while the perfume of the blue lavender in the centre will attract bees and lovers.

Jane Balsgaard's Lavender Passage *will, together with Jan Norman's* Beehive, *surely change the taste and colour of the honey produced in the area. Yet the* Lavender Passage *was in many ways a problematic structure. More than 1,000 lavenders had to be planted on the inclining interior sides of the structures built of pine and maple. Special nets had to be installed inside the two shapes in order to keep the earth from eroding, as well as pipes for watering in dry seasons. Also visitors sometimes cannot resist the temptation of taking the lavender home as a souvenir to be planted in their own gardens.*

Some works are intended to partici-pate in the natural process of decay without intervention, others, like Jane Balsgaard's need care and protection in order to survive. An agreement is necessary, between an organisation such as ours, and the artist, regarding responsibility in determining the lifespan of a particular work.

Alfio Bonanno

Lavender Passage, *1993,*
FROM ABOVE: Summer; Winter

JUSSI HEIKKILÄ
MIGRATION AVIUM

I dentifying oneself as part of the natural world is no less than a mental revolution, which is followed by an era of renewed values and a feeling of reverence. By depicting natural processes, ecological borderline states and Passion stories, Jussi Heikkilä wishes to create a spirited atmosphere of hope and action. *Hannu Castrén*

A natural starting point for me was to create a work based on birds: to collect information and personal experiences. I started in early June by bird-watching in the TICKON park. After seven days, I continued bird-watching in the Tranekær area. I also gathered information from local people and amateur ornithologists. Later on I consulted the Danish zoological museum in Copenhagen, and Finnish zoological museum in Helsinki.

I decided to take five levels in my work: personal, local, communal, national and globa. It was also an interesting starting point to know that it was the Danish school master, Hans Mortensen, who started organising modern bird-marking in 1899, in Viborg, Denmark.

After going through all the information, I chose eight directions for eight stones and scaled their distances. Every bird species I decided to take within the stones had to have been seen by myself in the area and furthermore had to be ring-marked in Denmark and then controlled in some other country. It was exciting to cross political, economical and religious borders with these birds.

The Finnish artist Jussi Heikkilä makes us aware that there are no national frontiers for birds. He is an ardent bird-watcher and has great knowledge in his field, travelling widely in order to make his observations. At TICKON he observed and registered the bird population, made long-distance calls to observation stations for further information and, at night, together with other visiting artists, practised owl calls to be answered from the dark trees. Alfio Bonanno

Migration Avium, *1993, details, two of the 8 stones*

CHRIS DRURY
COVERED CAIRNS

The cairns I make on walks in nature are made as marks for a special time and place. They are also an acknowledgement of something un-nameable beyond that, something which is in movement and perceived or seen. These cairns are not sculptures, they are simply pointing to something outside of the self and in movement. In a sense all my work does this. These cairns are built very simply, photographed, knocked down and then I walk on.

Since I do not make sculptures in the strict sense, this is a problem when I am asked to make a sculpture in a sculpture park. The perception of this 'thing in movement' is unpredictable, neither is 'special time' and place guaranteed, especially within domesticated spaces and where time is limited. At TICKON my intention was to cover or contain a cairn and thus mark what is within. The cairn points to inner nature. To allow an experience of this, the work is interactive. From outside, dome and cairn are a unified, defined object (sculpture) but when you enter the dome, the outside (the trees, sky, sounds, smells etc) are allowed in through the open weave and somehow enhanced. It is like looking out at nature from the position of a secure inner core.

Rather than make a work which points to something in nature seen through insight, I have decided to mirror the very process of nature. The dome is built in a marsh area and is made by pushing alternate hazel and willow wands into the ground. The willow is living and growing; the hazel is dead and will decay. The work will be allowed to go its own way, so I would predict eventually some boulders within a willow thicket. In other words I have imposed order (the dome is woven in a geometric form using a basket weave technique) which will revert to chaos, which in nature is the true order.

I came to TICKON at the end of April. The trees were still in bud, but the day I arrived was the start of a spring heatwave. Willow will not strike unless the wands are still in bud. We therefore had to hurriedly cut the willow and hazel from nearby and push the uprights into the ground. Three days later all the trees were in leaf! Nevertheless, most of the willow took. The work took nine days to make and the only help I needed was transporting and placing the two large boulders and cutting and transporting the willow and hazel.

Chris Drury's Covered Cairn *is a living work. Old building methods are combined with the knowledge of material and an instinctive way of working. From the beginning his work had to stand up to both sheep and visitors. The small stones within the dome often got knocked down, but as the artist predicted, people will keep putting them up again. He had left instructions to let the work look after itself.* Alfio Bonanno

Chris Drury, Covered Cairn, *1993, FROM ABOVE, L TO R: detail (the willows first delicate signs of life, the growing process has begun); Summer; Chris Drury working with* Covered Cairn, *1993; Winter*

39

ANDY GOLDSWORTHY

I use everything that I can, every thing! I think even the things that I have planned and given a tremendous amount of thought to, are only there to prime the spontaneity and the intuitiveness that is instinctively inside a thing. That ultimately is what drives my work. So even though I might consider what I am going to make and plan, it must in the end be driven by intuitiveness and instinct. Otherwise it won't work.

When I came here, I had no idea of what I was going to make. I did not know the place before I came, so I did not give a single thought to what I would make. The intention of my art is the artist's way of learning, of getting to know the place, my art teaches me about the land.

There is a tremendous undergrowth here, terrific undergrowth, and so many different grasses. Especially around the alder trees where there normally would be water, but this is now dried, so I can walk in there. But there are grasses in there that I have never worked with, that I have never come across: beautiful, beautiful grasses! And there is a lot of dead wood, debris wood – in many park areas that is taken away. And the trees have a strong presence, because they grow low to the ground. I made a piece where I wrapped a branch in grass, so it was almost like camouflage. It was interesting, the idea of grass becoming stick, becoming grass, becoming earth –

these things interest me.

Then I worked with the poppies, wrapped again round a stick in the field, so they are like partner-works. There is dark depth underneath the trees, almost like caves in the undergrowth. I think that making two sticks, one in the undergrowth and one on the edge of the park looking out to the field, is like dealing with those two different aspects of the place . . . The branch that I covered became like a red vein, pulsating red on the edge of the field. It was great.
From an interview with Astrid Gjesing, Tranekær, July 1993

During Andy Goldsworthy's first day at TICKON I felt his restlessness, he was eager to get to work. A few hours after his arrival he took his photography equipment and placed it in the middle of the driveway to the castle, just outside the artists' house. He then walked a few metres away from the camera and lay down patiently waiting for the rain he had sensed in the air. After several dry attempts, getting up and lying down, the rain finally came and in a few magic minutes the 'rain shadow' of Andy was left on the ground – a human mark existing only a few seconds.　　Alfio Bonnano

FROM ABOVE, L TO R: Iris Blade Poppy Wrapped, *1993;* Stick in Grass, *1993;* Poppy Wrapped Stick, *1993;* Rain Shadow, *1993, photos Andy Goldsworthy*

GIULIANO MAURI

THE AEOLIAN HARP

An installation consisting of six cones, one on top of the other, that twist upwards to reach an overall height of 15 metres. Each of the six cones, placed in a spiral sequence, is made of two thousand young, self-sown maple trees and has a free base. The great north wind that breathes life into the park is strong enough to move the sticks producing a deep sound in harmony with the natural environment. *Vittorio Fagone*

While the Aeolian Harp *was being built I overheard one visitor saying that had the state building inspector seen the process we would never have got permission to build it – an interesting point showing how important it is to have artists to build 'impossible' structures. Mauri, who was trained as a carpenter and builder, used a lot of steel wire and also nails to bind and secure the structure. This practice is considered almost offensive to those artists who shun materials alien to nature such as steel, plastic and cement. But what materials are truly natural?*

Situated by the lake the work is in line with and echoes the spire of Tranekær castle. Alfio Bonnano

Aeolian Harp, *1993, FROM ABOVE: Looking down at the internal structure which is solid enough to cope with strong winds; Winter; OPPOSITE, FROM ABOVE, L TO R: Summer; Autumn; The Aeolian Harp's basic structure raises skywards; Falling sticks are one of the working hazards for the faithful photographer!*

KAREN McCOY

STRUCTURES FOR DISCOURSE
ON LIGHT AND SHADE

Two structures, each 3.3 metres long, 1.5 metres wide and 2.4 metres high, were thatched with reeds collected in the immediate vicinity and constructed in a manner that honours local building practice. One is sited at the edge of a lake and oriented north-south, while the other is on a hilltop and oriented east-west. They are not visible one from the other but are connected by a path along an east-west axis. The path in the beech wood is approximately 150 x 2 metres. The structure on the lake site is empty, the one on the hilltop is filled with a rectangular mass of rammed earth.

I cannot say that I came to the site as a *tabula rasa*, because I brought my own personal history and history as a maker with me. I will say that I did not know what I would make when I arrived. The piece was formed out of a complex web of information, visual and verbal, found at the place.

Sources

Archaeology: Long houses found in archaeological excavations on Langeland, there is a question whether these houses were mortuaries or were used for domestic purposes. I like the idea of a structure of ambiguous function – a functional ambiguity that turns on life or death. My structures are long and narrow, loosely proportioned along the lines of these long houses and also built of materials indigenous to the island.

I was taken to see an eroding megalith site near Strandby. There within the eroding side of a large earthen mound one could see the remains of a 'stone bed' upon which would have laid the 'coffin' – possibly a hollow log.

Archaeological finds have revealed extensive grave hoards or votive offerings. For example, plant resources from a boat burial off Ærø (next to Langeland) included hazel nuts, acorns, empty cups and unripe fruits, stones of dogwood and hawthorn and seed of Fat Hen. Elm bark under the boat and fragments of the same piece over it indicate a 'wrapper'

for the boat and its contents. (*Journal of Danish Archaeology*, Volume #10, 1991.) *Grøn and Skaarup*, pp 45-6 – burials and sacrificial interments are mostly placed on an east-west axis, though some are north-south.

Geology: On the sea shores and in the fields there are special stones called Ledeblok or guide stones. These were deposited by the glaciers and knowledgeable friends have shown me which ones came from Norway for example, or from other places usually to the northeast of Langeland. I included some Ledeblok in the stone bed in the structure on the hilltop.

Hadebakker, glacial deposits made in holes in 'dead ice', form a characteristic landform of the visual environment on Langeland. These 'hat hills' are also referred to as 'maiden's breasts'. (I seem to have made a 'hat box' – I have raised the earth beneath the structure so we can see it clearly, the earth is itself no longer buried.)

Ecology/Biology: The island has a long history of human habitation – for approximately 6,000 years humans have been living on and out of this landscape. It has provided food and shelter continuously.

Visual Environment, Material Culture and Materials:

Agriculture – I had a strong attraction to the rolling fields of crops, to the barley, wheat and rape being cultivated. Cultivation is closely aligned with 'civilisation', it is seasonal and cyclical, temporary yet recurring.

Architecture – Shelter is tied to culture and civilisation, to human presence and activity on the landscape. The beauty and metaphorical possibility of thatching, which is part of the local architectural tradition, attracted me to it. I chose to emphasise the roof of the sculptural structures. A roof acknowledges (simply by its presence) the sky, the rain, the sun. Thatching uses materials at hand and is

said to have been (in some form) a means of shelter for as long as Denmark has been inhabited. The reeds must be harvested, organised – and stitched on to make a roof. A thatched roof is made by a slow incremental build-up, reed by reed, bundle by bundle. Reeds are harvested seasonally and have the potential to provide shade, insulation (from cold, heat and sound) and protection from other elemental forces. (Vulnerability is also expressed through the inherent threat of fire as a destructive force to this building material.) The reeds then grow up again the next season. At present there is no indication of depletion and the craft itself seems vital. The use of thatching provides a positive metaphor for the interaction of humans and nature.

Light – Langeland is a long, narrow island with a quality of light that is uniquely luminous and varied. This aspect affected siting choice.

Siting and Structure

Lake Site and Structure: The structure is tall, open and empty. The thickly-thatched roof has curved ends which function as an invitation to see in and through it. Its placement in the water causes the structure to act as an eco-shelter – in a literal sense it is more for birds, plants, earth and water than humans. The site within the growing reeds allows the structure to pay homage to the materials of its own making. It is also the *marker* of a 'trouble spot' – it permits the Borgsø to signify other endangered waters. The Castle Lake is itself unhealthy and out of balance.

The Walk and the View: The two structures are some distance apart. One cannot be seen from the other. Memory is called upon in order to see both structures. The walk between them is a time to ruminate. The east-west path culminates in a planted beech forest where the path leads along a 'spine' of cut trees. Within this planted grid it is dark and shadowy. The hilltop structure comes into view only

as the path makes its way uphill and to the east.

Hilltop Site and Structure: The walk opens out into the light and onto a view of the countryside and sea, there are the fields and farms – there is an old site for meetings of justice (the *folketing*) preserved as an 'island' in the wheat field. The structure is itself a site of (a particular kind of) human accumulation. It shelters a virtual wall of earth that is both protection and burial for its hidden contents. The edge of a stone bed is visible in some places along the outer walls. Placed on this embedded stone platform (within the solid mass of earth and unseen from the exterior) are crop plants, wild fruits and nuts and traditional Danish healing herbs. These are protected by a hollow log. Containers of water from the lake are buried in a small oval excavation underneath the whole structure. The roof of the structure on the hilltop has a protective straight-edged overhang, although it is expected that the rammed earth mass will be eroded in time, revealing its contents.

Collaboration and its Metaphors

It seems important to note that the project was realised as the result of collaboration between myself and several other individuals. For example, I learned a great deal from the thatcher, Arne Ludvigsen,

not only about the craft, but also about the history of thatching in Denmark. Our lengthy discussions about siting, materials, form and meaning had significant influence on the project. The biologists who helped me to understand the ecological condition of the lake, too, affected the depth and meaning of the work. I came to feel that the bringing together of the many disciplines in the project – art, craft, ecology, archaeology, geology, botany, history – was a metaphorical gesture meaningful in, and of, itself. This is especially the case within the context of our current segmented and fragmented cultural existence. The willingness to share, take risks and cross boundaries was significant.

Form and Language

The title is multivalent and I will only open the discussion here. Certainly daily and seasonal cycles are referred to, as well as perception – seeing and not seeing. The title suggests that the two go together, light and shade, that is, and that the artwork itself conducts the discourse. There is that upon which light is cast – the structures refer to the condition of the earth. The simple presence of the structures sheds light on their sites. There is the shade cast by the shelter itself, but shade may also be thought of as obscuring, as mysterious. Casting light on mystery illuminates its presence but does

not necessarily expose or undo it.

The American artist Karen McCoy stayed at TICKON for over a month, carrying out geological, biological, archaeological and historical research of the area. Many local experts willingly offered time and experience. The influence of the many thatched roofs on our island is evident in her two Structures for Discourse on Light and Shade. *The title has its roots in the first structure built in the lake under a group of alders where the midday sun passing through the leaves caresses her structure with passages of light. A local thatcher, Arne Ludvigsen offered to help her and many bundles of reeds had to be found, harvested and dried. By incorporating local handicraft, tradition and materials, Karen has made her work appeal to a large public. The structures have, after half a year, begun their process of decay. With time they will reveal their 'ritual' contents. I feel the element of time a most relevant issue when talking of Art-Nature expressions, the process of life, growth and decay.*

Alfio Bonanno

Structure(s) for Discourse on Light and Shade, *1993, two structures, OPPOSITE, FROM ABOVE, L TO R: Hilltop Site, Summer; Autumn; Winter; Lake Site, Winter, PAGE 44: Lake Site, Summer*

tickon

DAVID NASH

SHEEP SPACES

An environmental work engages aspects of the life of a particular location – that active engagement being the meaning of the work. A sculpture placed in the environment is not the same as a sculpture made 'of' the active elements of the environment.

Looking for an appropriate work for TICKON I found a copse of trees that the resident flock of sheep used to shelter from the sun and rain. Coming from a region of sheep – North Wales – I noticed the sheep did not have any 'spaces' – wall, rock, hedge, bank, fallen tree, to nestle against. These spaces are noticeable in sheep regions, spaces where the sheep continually go to rest and shelter. They do not make the spaces, no digging or shaping, just their continual presence wears an oval patch, an egg-shaped space – peaceful, innocent and holy.

Eight large tree-pieces were moved into the copse and arranged in pairs. The sheep knew what they were for immediately and were using the first pair when we came back with the second.

Some of the environmental works at TICKON had been fenced to keep the sheep out, the sheep being an essential part of this sculpture solved that problem. The continued life of this sculpture is determined by the presence of the sheep.

The first artist to be approached was David Nash. He was very busy but I could feel that he sensed, through my phone-call, the seriousness and urgency of our need for his participation in the TICKON project. He agreed to come and help us and has since returned several times. In the summer of 1993, he spent two weeks at TICKON where he created his Sheep Spaces as well as his Burnt Oak installation for the Kunsthallen Brandts Klædefabrik, Odense, the first major presentation of his work in Scandinavia.

David's stay at TICKON was a great experience for all that worked with him. Just the way in which he chose a piece of wood and proceeded to shape it with his chainsaw showed the perception and hand of a master. Also very special was the collaboration between David and his helpers, his patience and the way he made them participate. He gave himself time to talk to them, to explain and to thank them after a day's work. They respected him and his work, even though some did not quite understand what he was doing. Alfio Bonanno

Sheep Spaces, *1993, FROM ABOVE, L TO R: Spaces which give the sheep shelter, protection and a place to rest; David Nash working on the fallen oak for* Sheep Spaces, *Autumn; Winter*

JAN NORMAN
BEEHIVE

My aim was to create a quiet piece of civilisation in a hidden or even undiscovered space. Built with materials from the wood and with the help of noble craftsmen, born by tradition. A connection which touches upon a solemn and mythical character. A place for bees.

As when a scream breaks a silence, when the unexpected, the unforeseen tears us out of the sleeping habitual life.

While David Nash took the sheep into consideration for his work, the Danish artist Jan Norman catered for the bees. He built a thatched, five-metre high beehive. The alliance with local helpers was necessary in order to build the wooden structure from which to suspend the huge hive as well as for the construction of the thatched hive itself. Norman also had to appeal to local bee specialists to make sure that his idea of installing a hive of bees would succeed. He chose his materials with the greatest care, deeply involved in the process, including the choice of special plants to be sown under the hive in order to attract the bees that will be installed in the spring. They will surely act as guardians of the work and keep the many visitors at a safe distance. Alfio Bonanno

Beehive, *1993, FROM ABOVE, L TO R:*
Summer; Working on Beehive, *1993;*
Autumn; Winter

50

LARS VILKS
TEXTUS

Made out of both large and small branches of wood at the beginning of June 1993, *Textus* is a process work, connecting several different processes, built around an old tree which was probably hit by a thunderstorm. The tree is still alive and will keep growing into the structure. It also attracts a large audience as you can enter the work and walk and climb in it. Thirdly the work will be continued: although it is already quite a large piece, the ambition is to make it much bigger.

The piece is 90 per cent the work of one man, who has developed a method of construction with almost no experience of building at all. It is the result of a trial and error method used since 1980. There are already two constructions of the same type, *Nimis* (owned by Christo and placed in a nature reserve in the south of Sweden, about 200 metres in length) and *Marsyas* (about 50 metres in length) in Stockholm. All pieces are continually being worked at.

The construction work is extremely physical, the parts are connected and made strong through heavy nailing. *Textus* in its present state took six working days to build (12-hour working days).

The Swedish artist and art historian Lars Vilks came to TICKON for six days, worked like one obsessed, used thousands of nails, ripped his clothes in the process, got blisters on his hands and, before leaving us caught a bad cold. His three-storey high architectural construction attracts lots of visitors who enter its heart at the risk of falling down or breaking a leg. And Vilks is coming back over the next few years in order to build on to his Textus.   Alfio Bonanno

Textus, *1993, FROM ABOVE:*
Summer; Winter

HELGE RØED

WOOD AND WATER
A Space Exploration

An important part of man's orientation to nature attaches to an identification of the forces that are in the materials themselves. In projects of nomadic character, I have always found it interesting to concentrate energy on psychic charging of an area in a limited period of time.

Helge Røed

Many artists working 'exclusively' with natural materials nevertheless include well-camouflaged alien materials, while others use huge machines and power tools in order to produce their 'nature' art. There are questions of terminology and professionalism in this field that need analysis and unravelling. In this piece, which caused the most controversy at TICKON, Norwegian artist Helge Røed quite intentionally used yellow plastic pipes. These were placed horizontally among the trees next to the lake and when seen from a distance they formed a perfect oval, reflecting the shape of the lake.

However a lady, very upset, said to me that she could not understand or accept these plastic pipes in nature. 'It would', in her opinion, 'have been much more natural to use painted wood, which after all, was a natural material.' This, I felt, was a misunderstanding. Stripping a piece of wood of its identity and painting it to make it look like plastic, instead of making use of real plastic,

would have been a misuse of a natural material. A material should be chosen for its language and identity. Helge Røed very carefully chose the colour of his plastic to fit in exactly with the natural colours of the environment. Imported from Norway, as Denmark did not have pipes of the right colour, they were yellow with green reflections like the flowers of dandelions growing underneath them. After four seasons the pipes will be removed in accordance with the artist's wishes.   Alfio Bonanno

Wood and Water (A Space Exploration), *1993, FROM ABOVE, L TO R: Autumn; Work in progress; Winter, the contentious yellow pipes, now covered in snow, blend in with nature, uniting the natural with manmade objects*

54

JØRN RØNNAU
THE UNICORN

Walking the wild-growing parkland and forest at TICKON for two days, I became fascinated by the large amount of honeysuckle growing in the forest, forcing the young trees to twist and grow in spiral-like shapes.

Some months earlier I had been considering the idea of making a unicorn's horn carved out of a tree, still rooted in its natural surroundings, but there had been no right opportunity, no right tree, and no right environment so far. Seeing all these honeysuckles brought the idea back to me, but I did not really consider it to be realistic, because too many things had to be right.

The unicorn is a unique product of human imagination. An archetype, maybe. Out in nature – as you may know – the unicorn is extremely shy and cannot normally be seen! On rare occasions, though, you might seem to sense its presence! The legend tells us that if a virgin goes out alone into the forest and lies down and falls asleep, the unicorn will come and put his head in her lap. When she takes hold of the horn, it becomes docile and follows her!

The site had to have the isolated secrecy of that legend. It also had to have a big and straight tree that was not growing vertically.

On the third day, I was walking through a dry, rather wet area with mixed vegetation, alder and a few, very old oak trees loosing huge dead branches. Right in front of me the forest opened into a small glade next to a marshy area with reeds. On the edge of this marsh, one of the old oak trees had been turned halfway over, many years ago in a storm, but it continued to grow, attempting to stabilise itself. Not very successfully, though, because the crown was growing too, weighing it down into the marsh. By taking down the crown and making the tree into a sculpture, I could save it from falling. Being oak it might still stand for another 50 years or more.

Carving it was an immense physical and spiritual challenge, I was very happy living and working in that place for weeks. I got to know the animals there – the deer, the fox, the wren, the lizard and all the others – even with the noise of my chain saw. I saw the changes in the weather, the movement of the sun, its light shaping the spiral of the *Unicorn*, making it turn. I saw it pointing at the local couple of common buzzards spiralling in the air. I saw it pointing at passing seagulls and jetplanes drawing white lines. And in the evening I saw it pointing at the stars, of course, just as star moss is growing on its roots!

The Unicorn *created by the Danish artist Jørn Rønnau, is a poetical addition to TICKON. In this work the question of whether or not to sacrifice a living oak for the sake of art has arisen several times. It is an important question and keeps on surfacing. Would it be more morally correct to use a dead tree? Are we hurting nature? Interesting to note, that by these reactions we associate (identify) ourselves with nature and define our relationship to it. Like Rønnau, most artists working in nature today are very much aware of its living elements and nurture great respect, yet there are some who use natural elements only as a working material, regardless, for creating their work.*   Alfio Bonanno

tickon

Unicorn, 1993, FROM ABOVE, L TO R: Jørn Rønnau beginning the first stages of work on Unicorn; Summer; Autumn; Winter

ALAN SONFIST

MAZE OF THE GREAT OAK OF DENMARK WITHIN STONE SHIP
1001 Young Trees

A beautifully formed oak leaf, placed in stones and surrounded by an immense stone ship. This is a work which immediately activates the idea of our forefathers, the Vikings and ship building. The stone ship symbolises the past. The oak-tree is of great importance in Norse mythology and history, therefore the oak leaf is in the middle and when the work with the stones is entirely finished, small oak trees will be planted as a symbol of the future . . . For Alan Sonfist the position of the piece is not the only important condition, it is of vital importance that the art work suits the chosen society – both culturally as well as archaeologically. He is always looking for suitable places for making art, places which unite the past, the present, the future and nature. At the same time it must suit the human beings on the spot. It is necessary that they like it as art, but must also that they feel the art work suits and belongs to the place.' (Øboon, 1993)

Alan Sonfist came to TICKON with his wife and baby daughter Rebecca Oakleaf who was only a few months old, so while working at his maze he also undertook his share of baby sitting. The position of this extremely large piece was chosen with great care. Much of the work was done, when one moonlit night he went out and changed the position of the leaf. This caused confusion among the workers the next day but also showed them the seriousness of his intentions. It had to be just right in place and form. Within the contours, several hundred small oak saplings have been planted, while the veins are marked by stones. In time the oakleaf will become oaktrees, in homage to the prehistoric oaks that once covered Denmark. Alfio Bonanno

The Maze of the Great Oak of Denmark within Stone Ship – 1001 Young Trees, *1993, FROM ABOVE, L TO R: Count Preben Ahlefeldt-Laurvig (left) talking to Alan Sonfist during the 'mapping' of the maze, Summer 1993; Detail of the maze with its stone borders and the newly-planted oak trees which symbolise an optimistic future; Summer; Winter, during a storm*

tickon

57

NILS UDO

Sketching with flowers. Painting with clouds. Writing with water. Tracing the wind in May, the path of a falling leaf. Working for a thunderstorm. Awaiting a glacier. Bending the wind. Straightening out water and light. The May-green call of the cuckoo, the invisible tracing of its flight path. Space. The cry of an animal. The bitter taste of the daphne. Burying the pond and the dragon fly. Setting fire to the fog and the perfume of the yellow berberis. Marrying sounds, colours and smells. The green grass. Counting a forest and a meadow.

1972. A concrete, living, three-dimensional space in nature should be unlocked with the smallest possible interference and, if possible, only one focal point, to be transformed, under tension, into a work of art. Space and time, earth, water, fire, air, dead and living matter could become the trigger or theme for a work of art. I attached great value to this aspect from the very beginning. Many of my works resulted from plantings.

Anything that man can perceive with his five senses is part of the conception. The nature site should be experienced by seeing, hearing, smelling, tasting and feeling: also as a kind of Utopian comprehensive work of art, born from nature and sinking back into her.

A defined section of a nature site has simply been reorganised, ie: the existing materials have been put into a different order. A temporary reorganisation of course: one day it will have vanished, taken back by nature without trace.

In 1978 I wrote about the construction of my first big nest on the Luneburg Heath, made from birches and earth: 'I smelt the earth, the stones, the freshly cut wood. I built up the walls and plaited the floor of the nest. I looked down from the high rim of the nest onto the forest floor, into the interwoven branches of the trees and to the sky. I listened to the birdsong and was touched by the breath of the wind. At dusk I felt cold. Squatting high up on the nest's rim I thought: 'The nest is not yet ready; I am building myself a house that sinks silently through the tree tops down to the forest floor, it is open to the cold night sky, but it is still warm and soft, dug deep into the dark earth'. The archetypal character of a nest. An image that represents the attempt to overcome all painful separations and categories in the all-fusing furnace of a creative act.

Nature is still complete and inexhaustible in her most remote refuges, her magic still real. At any time, meaning any season, in all weathers, in things great and small. Always. Potential Utopias are under every stone, on every leaf and behind every tree, in the clouds and in the wind. Sensations are omnipresent. As a realist I only need to grasp them. To redeem them from their anonymity. Through the idiotic and ineradicable belief in Utopia. Pitting poetry against the inhuman river of time. (Nobody nowadays is interested. The subject of nature is *passé* – except for the Greens who can no longer tell an oak from a beech.)

A basic idea of the work was the attempt at absolute purity. Nature should, so to speak, present itself as on a stage. Any unnatural element was excluded as impure. This meant that only materials belonging to any given nature site were being used. It was their characteristics, the appropriate possibilities they offered and the character of the site itself that largely determined the shape of my work. This restriction as well as working in ever new nature sites and discovering ever new materials led to ever new results. It became apparent that the overwhelming mass of natural phenomena could mostly only be worked on in minute fragments taken out of their context.

Documentation of a dying world experience. To bear witness, at the last possible moment, to a now seemingly anachronistic perception of life, an attitude that can barely be understood, even by those willing to do so.

Of course many pretend to love nature. Just as everybody wants peace. But in reality they lost contact with nature long ago. They no longer see her, let alone hear or smell, taste or feel her. And if (sometimes) they do look, they don't see her: they have lost the ability to take a wider view of nature, in the sense both of space and time.

Even if I work alongside nature, preparing my intrusions as gently as possible, they always remain a basic contradiction within themselves. My whole work rests on this contradiction. It does not escape the inherent destiny of our existence. It injures what it touches: nature's virginity.

Realising the latent potential in nature, turning Utopia into reality: that which has never formally existed, but always been inherently there. A lifespan of a second is enough. The event has taken place.

Turning nature into art? Where is the critical dividing line between nature and art? This does not interest me. What counts for me is that my actions, Utopia-like, fuse life and art into each other. Art does not interest me. My life interests me. My reaction to events that shape my existence. Might there be friends of the arts interested in my life? *1978/93*

Like Andy Goldsworthy's work, Nils Udo's pieces at TICKON were ephemeral. They both create the seemingly irrational out of petals, berries etc making us aware of the exquisite detail by the unexpected juxtapositions. Through their photographic registrations the frozen images are handed down for us to participate in their dialogue with nature. They capture time and make it stop. Time that gives us the seasons of human existence – night and day, life and death – the eternal cycles in which our participation is of a very limited duration. Yet it is by time that we measure so much of what we do and on which we are totally dependent.

Alfio Bonanno

FROM ABOVE, L TO R: Moss Cushion with Rowanberries, 1993; The Place of the Rowanberries, 1993, Red Beech with Rowanberries, 1993, Eiche Flügelnuss, 1993, photos Nils Udo

BROR WESTMAN

BONE TAPESTRY

When I first visited the Tranekær area, about one year before the opening of TICKON, I was shown the gibbet hill and was told that here they executed the last man hanged in Denmark. For a long time I had wanted to make something with bones because of their sound. On my visit to Tranekær I visited a friend and in his garden door I saw a carpet of wooden pearls keeping the flies out in the hot summer air and rattling in the breeze. There I got the idea to make a bone carpet for the gibbet hill. My background is home-made musical instruments, sound sculptures and aeolian harps. The bone carpet had to rattle with a real gibbet hill sound.

For a whole year I collected bones. People in Langeland were asked to collect bones, my friends started to collect for me, some people sent me bones from their summer residence – little parcels with bones. On Midsummer Day in my home area we had three lambs grilled and I asked my friend there to keep the bones for me.

For nearly a year I worked with bones, hanging them outside in order to make them beat against each other and rattle in the wind. They became better and better while drying in the air.

Two problems had to be solved. Which sort of wire is flexible and strong enough? And, could we get enough bones? As time passed I was getting more and more nervous. The report from Langeland told

of too few bones in spite of the fact that all schools were asked to collect bones for me. At last we decided to buy bones. The local butcher sold us bones from oxen and pigs and they were kept in cold storage until my arrival. Next problem: they had meat on them. We had very little time and we decided to boil the bones, but what would be big enough to boil them in? Fortunately a farm nearby belonging to Tranekær Castle had a big copper pot.

When I arrived at Tranekær with my wife in order to work with the bones, I got a shock when I saw the magnitude and size of the bones. I was accustomed to supermarket-size bones and not real natural bones. The supermarket bones we had collected shrunk to nothing.

We boiled bones for three days and nights. I decided that the carpet should have the form of a wing symbolising both air and sound. It should be about five metres wide and hang from a log suspended in chains from the bough of one of the largest trees on the hill, a small-leafed maple. The longest chain of bones should have been about three metres long and the smallest only about one metre. When we arrived at the top of the hill we had to shorten the log for aesthetic and practical reasons, so now it is less than five metres long.

In a barn nearby, I laid all the bones out on the floor in the right form and connected them, through holes at both ends

of the big bones, with wire in rows in order to fasten them to the log on the hill.

The winter storms show us that the problem still is the strength and flexibility of the wire.

I still collect bones when I find them on a walk along the sea, and I still keep the bones from our supermarket meals.

One of the most striking things about doing this piece was the enthusiastic involvement from all the schools and kindergartens on Langeland who helped us find the many bones needed for the curtain, even though after a few months of open-air biology classes the result was a few fragile bird bones. We then had to go out and buy over one thousand pounds of prime soupbones that had to be cooked and prepared for the hanging. During this process there was a tremendous odour in the area around the boiling site. Despite some problems with the wire, the bones are beginning to rattle and move as they dry and the piece is reaching maturity. Alfio Bonanno

Bone Tapestry, *1993, FROM ABOVE, L TO R: Collecting the bones from the local supermarket; Summer; Autumn; Winter*

GIULIANO MAURI

ART IN NATURE 1981-1993
Vittorio Fagone

The year 1993 was marked by two out of the ordinary international events which favour the recent tendency for precise locations for exhibiting and producing creative work. They are emblematic of a new climate which in my opinion is, at the end of the century, setting the scene for radically different expressions of artistic creativity.

One of the events, at Tranekær in Denmark, on the island of Langeland, is located in a 300,000 square-metre area of parkland, that is, with its variety of landscapes, among the largest and most evocative of Northern Europe. The other is at Tagebau Greifenhain, on a vast open-cast coal mine in Niederlausitz between Berlin and Dresden. On these two sites several artists, who have worked for years on the creation of installations set in the natural environment, had the chance to present a significant part of their work. Essential features of this work include the use of natural materials, the return to basic cultural techniques and the absolute and untransferable fusion with the site for which the works are planned. The most striking fact about this creative work, in which each artist employs his own techniques and strategies, is that it overcomes the *historical* opposition between art and nature in favour of a different and harmonious alliance with nature.

Giuliano Mauri is an artist who, alone in Italy, has been working in this direction for more than a decade. For the two events in question he produced two remarkably complex and interesting works of art that deserve to be described because they clearly demonstrate his singular creative practice.

The *Arpa eolica* (Aeolian harp) at Tranekær is an installation consisting of six cones, one on top of the other, that twist upwards to reach an overall height of 15 metres. Each of the six cones, placed in a spiral sequence, is made of 2,000 young self-sown maple trees and has a free base. The great North wind that breathes life into the park is strong enough to move the sticks producing a deep sound in harmony with the natural environment. Situated on the edge of a lake between tall oaks, the work is in line with the castle of the Counts of Ahlefeldt-Laurvig on the opposite shore. In this setting, this vegetal construction of Giuliano Mauri reveals itself as a solid and calculated weave of natural materials, an optical machine, producing a lively reverberation of

signs in the countryside and forming a landmark seen in sweeping panoramic views.

The installation in the Greifenhain mine area is complex. The connection with the site is full of meaning that expands on a symbolic level. Greifenhain is in fact the scene of a sort of 'ecological genocide'. In 1936, the creation of an open-cast coal mine that has now reached a depth of 85 metres, led to the systematic destruction of one of the largest German forests. Approximately ten million trees have been sacrificed in this industrial operation and the mining of coal, by eliminating all trace of water from the ground, has turned an area of approximately 340 square kilometres into a sort of 'desert'.

Giuliano Mauri managed to find the traces in the ground of an ancient medieval church on the edge of this area. The church had been transferred, stone by stone, to another location 30 kilometres away in the 1930s. The artist consequently started to erect a gigantic *Cattedrale vegetale* (Vegetal cathedral) on the same site. In this project the materials he normally uses, branches pruned from trees, are joined together to form genuine pillars that rise to a height of 12 metres, and then curve like Gothic arches for another three metres. The 'pillars', arranged in pairs, trace the outline of arcades like the vaults of a Gothic nave.

The former inhabitants of the area, now dispersed in nearby towns, recognised the historical and religious significance of Giuliano Mauri's work and all agreed that they wanted to support the artist throughout the entire project. At present this has only just begun with the building of the front of the construction. In both these cases Giuliano Mauri interprets the uniqueness and humanity of the countryside he finds. The constructions are not only bound to the environment but also succeed in specifying its look and feel.

These two recent and fortunate excursions to Northern Europe should not allow us to forget the scenery that the artist visits with almost obsessive daily regularity. Giuliano Mauri lives in Lodi and knows, down to its innermost secrets, the forms and make-up and the seasonal changes of the attractive surrounding countryside and its river, the Adda. It is above all the environment of the River Adda that for ten years has constituted this artist's *workshop* and the ever-changing *gallery* for his original work.

L'albero dei cento nidi (*The tree of a hundred nests*), Lodi, 1992

Giuliano Mauri first came to *art in nature* at the beginning of the 80s. Until then, Giuliano Mauri had worked within the sphere of the 'militant' poetry movement which directed its attention towards the social and political environment. After 1968 and for much of the 70s it was heavily involved in experimentation aimed at more direct expressive communication in Italy, France and Germany.

The first work that can be classified as belonging to the anthropological and environmental dimension of art in nature was *La casa dell'uomo raccoglitore* (The home of man the harvester) that Giuliano Mauri produced in the grounds of the church of Sant'Agostino in Bergamo Alta. It is a complex construction occupying a space of 12 x 24 x 12 metres in volume and is made from branches, canvas, wood, rope and mud. It is in some ways a work that presents a manifesto: in a primary and historical dimension, man the harvester decides to settle down in one place, tying himself to the land rather than moving about with the other hunters; he will be able to live off it and with it, modifying it according to his productive capabilities and his own subjective needs. At the same time, man the harvester establishes a new boundary for his habitat, which, however, is never out of harmony with the vast natural environment.

The works on the River Adda were done in the same year. These were more specifically oriented towards a new poetic style. The artist gave them the title *Codici acquatici* (Aquatic codes) and in them, sticks taken from locust trees depict a variety of continuous signs that are like the letters or ideograms of a natural alphabet. At this point the beginnings can already be seen of a choice then becomes an unchanging rule throughout the subsequent work of Giuliano Mauri: a new image in the countryside can only be created properly if materials belonging to that same countryside are used in its creation. It is interesting to note that a process of reviving basic manufacturing techniques began at this time. The use of branches pruned from trees as construction material and weaving techniques to give structural form is an effective means that is plastic and meaningful.

A second and decisive element of his poetic style is defined in *La scala del paradiso* (The staircase of heaven) of 1982. This too was designed for the natural habitat of the River Adda. Here a long ladder in the form of a spiral rises from the banks and the water of the river towards the sky. It seems at this point to express a natural contemplating religious tension that is concrete on an earthly scale. These great emblems, these woven branches that the artist is to use more and more in subsequent years, are the achievements of a vision open to wider and freer outlooks. They are a recognisable expression of an acute sense of time. The sky appears physically dense and variable, not remote. It becomes another pole of

attraction for each and every vegetal form and dialogue with the earth.

This natural religious aspect becomes explicit in the *Altari vegetali* (Vegetal altars) of 1983, produced in the country near Lodi. These are singular constructions in which a horizontal level, raised but close to the ground, contrasts with an articulated vertical structure of branches and tree trunks. These constructions show how the vegetable world can use intertwined and live branches with support elements to carve out a plastic dimension that both mirrors and anticipates movements of life. In that same year, Giuliano Mauri produced *Zeppelin vegetale* (Vegetal Zeppelin), a creation that identifies another important passage in his work. In this creation, the weaving and intertwining of branches and sticks is now directed towards the structural definition of a spherical or oval closed form that one can see through. The definition of the form can be seen at every moment of its constitution and the form is never impaired.

Giuliano Mauri laid out *La città del sole* (The city of the sun) on the banks of the Adda in 1984. This complex vegetal installation sets off an ordered geometrical gridwork of sticks and branches, cleverly assembled in rhythmic patterns against the free and vital expansion of the woods, as if to emphasise the two possible ways and modalities of inhabiting nature today.

In 1985, at the international exhibition 'Milanopoesia', filmed by Gianni Sassi, examples of 'weaving of the woods' were successfully presented as models of original research in the area of visual languages. The *Isole vaganti* (Drifting islands), 1985, have a unique charm. They link the transparent bed of the irrigation canals typical of the Lodi countryside, to the liquid surface of the water by means of a light and fluctuating network of woven structures and the drifting surfaces of aquatic plants and leaves.

In 1986 Giuliano Mauri planned the construction, in the woods, of a large church consisting entirely of tall natural structures that soar upwards. In that year he was given the chance, thanks to the cooperation of the Centro Internazionale di Brera, to construct this work of art in the deconsecrated church of San Carpoforo in Milan, occupying the whole of it. The result was both exciting and involving, a real forest of carefully arranged sticks depicting a Gothic structure in a church of baroque design. In the rarefied space of the church, each of the vegetal segments became a matrix of vivid signals and at the same time the expression of a procreative and structuring force. The apse was occupied by an enormous cylindrical body with a wide weave and a spiralling aerial walkway allowing one to pass from the ground almost up to the vault. The contrast between the high stone walls and the solid complex of the wooden structure appeared

both paradoxical and logical at the same time. At no point do the woven branches sag and touch the solid perimeter of the masonry but neither do they contradict it: they both thrust upwards. The 'wooden church' is only more earthly and human. It is consistent with a dimension of transient temporality which is that of the whole natural universe explored by the artist.

The guiding principles of Giuliano Mauri's work seem to be clearly determined by the second half of the 80s. In the environmental dimension, his creations seem, from one work to the next, to aim at two goals: to identify the terms of a possible way of creating forms that do not put a distance between nature and manual craftsmanship and to establish perceptual lines and genuine paths in the countryside that create an optical involvement in people walking them and, more generally, just to increase their visual sensitivity. *Le trombe di paradiso* (The trumpets of paradise) created in the countryside near Mantua in 1987, should be interpreted from this point of view. They are material vegetal constructions where the shape of a trumpet, clearly alluded to, develops on a very full scale. Again it is of an earthly nature. Similarly the walks of the *Fiume vestito* (Dressed river) animate the fluvial countryside of Marecchia with an alarmed and actively involved scene and then there are the *Canti dell'esilio d'occidente* (Songs of Western exile) dense with vegetal fabrics that can be walked on. Both these works were created in 1988, at Sant'Arcangelo di Romagna. That year two episodes occurred that show the opposite poles of the creative horizon of this artist. Giuliano Mauri deposited some *Spore vegetali* (Vegetal spores) in the park of Villa Barzino at Busalla (Genoa). These were artefacts obtained by intertwining branches which suggest closed geometrical shapes; they are spores to the extent that they have been transferred and are transferable, like procreative nuclei.

By this time the scale of the artist's work in the area of the Adda, covered greater and greater areas, entire islets in the river. Giuliano Mauri dedicated himself to a *Tessitura del bosco* (Weaving of the woods). He joins live vegetal elements, structural supports and woven surfaces in a single fabric which never sours the environmental context but exalts it with its tangibility and visibility. The manual creativity of the artist seeks a profound agreement with nature and experiments with modulating the emblems of this 'alliance' that has been rediscovered

In 1991, at Monteciccardo (Pesaro), Giuliano Mauri attempted to tie together the two opposite poles of his work into a new dimension. *L'albero* (The tree), loaded with sphere-shaped vegetal artefacts hung on branches, seems to exalt its own generous, hospitable and productive presence. While the patient work on the 'weaving of the woods' continued during this period on the

banks and small islands of the Adda, in 1992 the design for *L'albero dei cento nidi* (The tree of a hundred nests) began to take shape on what is probably the scale and in the context most truly his. A gigantic oak, isolated in the open country-side near Lodi is loaded by the artist with woven vegetal artefacts each of which is different. In spring and summer they are partly camouflaged by the leafy bows of the tree, giving it a unique appearance during the snowy winter months. Metaphor and appearance do not seem distant from each other here. Without any need to look elsewhere, *L'albero dei cento nidi* is a definite presence and an immediately recognisable icon.

In 1992 the two *Torri vegetali* (Vegetal towers) were produced for 'Arte Sella' in the alpine countryside near Borgo Valsugana (Trent). These two installations, again on the edge of a wood, rise up through the tops of the trees. The solid geometry of the woven structures contrasts with the trees and hazardous routes upwards can be discovered inside the geometry. From inside the towers the immediately surrounding countryside acquires a plastic appearance that changes at different heights like fluid form.

Certain aspects of Giuliano Mauri's creative development deserve further emphasis. Above all there is his keen awareness of the changes, the eclipses and rebirth of a countryside he explores every day. Rarely has the countryside around Lodi and the scenery of the Adda had such a closely involved interpreter. The work of the artist exalts the terms of a new way of seeing that sees equally well both close to and in distant perspective and chooses as its field of observation, that very variable field of the natural horizon.

Manual skill returns here to its primary state. Furthermore, the distance that separates material culture tied to the manufacture of consumer objects, from artistic culture which expands on a symbolic level, is completely upset here. The artist demonstrates how one can *write nature* without hiding behind remote points of view.

Finally, Giuliano Mauri discovers the concrete forms of abstract concepts in the countryside in which he lives and outlines two fundamental parameters of humanisation for the spectator who wants to follow him. He outlines the *awareness of time*, of its passing and its rise and fall with the seasons and a *natural piety*, not foreign, that is the mirror image of this awareness.

The sense of nature that characterises the end of our century definitely does not set culture against nature but appeals to a *culture of nature* and the work of the artist in its most advanced expressions and perspicacity is witness to this, and certainly proof of it.

Tessitura del bosco *(Weaving of the woods), 1987*

68

DAVID NASH
THE LANGUAGE OF WOOD
Gertrud Købke Sutton

Lying on the floor of the Columnless Hall at Kunsthallen Brandts Klædefabrik is a tree. The trunk and limbs are stripped of bark, exposing veins and knots. It is cut into pieces and the ends of the trunk pieces are split open so that they gape. They resemble mouths, snouts and elephant lips. Boat-shaped pieces of branch lie between the lips. They are caught in the gaping splits; or perhaps they have forced the wood apart? There are energies which both expand and contract and that pull the dismembered tree together into one large, organic interdependence. The wood is burnt black where limb and trunk meet. This links them together. The charred light from the burns changes from deep black to a slight tint, while the wood itself is warm and light. The pieces of trunk are stripped naked and the 'boats' have cut surfaces on two sides. A rhythm like a pulse beat or breathing runs through the composition. Each part is autonomous, but connected. This is how David Nash works. He considers each detail, each work and all the works as part of a process: 'I want a life and work that reflects the balance and continuity of nature Identifying with the time and energy of the tree and with its morality, I find myself drawn deeper into the joys and blows of nature. Worn down and regenerated; broken off and reunited; a dormant faith revived in the new growth of old wood'. This, his credo 20 years ago, sounds the same today. One work leads to another like the chords in a measure and the movements in a symphony.

This is the first time Englishman David Nash, a pioneer among Land Art artists, has worked in Denmark. He and ten other like-minded artists from near and far were invited to work at Tranekær Internationale Center for Kunst og Natur (TICKON) on the island of Langeland. The show at Brandts was made specifically for that space but is as well a part of his work for TICKON. The material is from Langeland and the preparations and charring have taken place out in the open, but with the measurements and light of the Columnless Hall in mind. Nearly all of David Nash's sculptures, including the large number in museums, have been prepared outdoors. It's a question of proportion and scale.

Nash considers himself part of the second generation of artists who work in nature with nature. The first generation includes artists such as Robert Smithson, Robert Morris, Michael Heizer, and others. They broke with the commercial gallery world in the early 60s and moved their activities into nature. They chose remote areas and inaccessible places in deserts and mountains, but their constructions were not always sensitive to nature as such. Often large amounts of rock and earth had to be moved. Since then there has been a change in attitude due to the seriousness of the environmental situation. The concept of work in nature has broadened, aesthetics and ethics have become unified and new challenges now delineate the art.

Nature has always played a very important role in English art, both as inspiration and metaphor. The artists of the interwar and postwar periods, Henry Moore, Barbara Hepworth and Graham Sutherland, blended surrealistic tendencies with traditional English romanticism of nature. David Nash is tarred with same brush. In 1967 he made the epoch-making and romantic decision to move to an unromantic environment which he had known as a child. Blaenau Ffestiniog is a small, grey Welsh village set in the slate mountains, the quarries now shut down. For little money he converted a high-ceilinged, Palladian former chapel into his studio and bought two small houses and a piece of land.

Dialogue with Wood

In Wales he began his long discourse with wood both as a sculptural material and as a living, growing thing. He chopped and planted and with experience he learned to yield to the signals of the wood. Originally, he polished his wooden sculptures. They became more his as the birthmarks vanished. He thought that one had to polish, but hated it, 'and they cracked anyway'. That seemed a problem. In 1973 he wrote in connection with a show entitled 'Briefly Cooked Apples': 'Three rows of three – all cut from one trunk – they crack and live on – they split and let their souls fly out'. The nature of wood is its idiom. The connotation of the chainsaw is one of destruction, but all metal tools – axe, wedge, chisel are harder than wood, and all wooden sculptures deal with resistance. The degrees of hardness and resistance in the various types of wood are part of their quality, their essence. The existence of each thing and creature deals with its ability to resist. Oak seems to throw the saw out and birch is different according to where it grows. In Japan

FROM ABOVE: David Nash working on his sculpture for the Burnt Oak installation at Kunsthallen, Brandts Klædefabrik, Odense, 1993; Charring the sculptures for the Burnt Oak installation, 1993

FROM ABOVE: David Nash in The Ash Dome; Seven Charred Shapes, *1989, Oak, 500 x 600cm;* Threshold Column, *1990, charred elm in progress*

it is quite another tree than in Europe: 'They said it was birch. I thought they had got the name wrong. Then I thought there was something wrong with the saw. Then I got my chisel out – and realised it was just this incredibly hard type'. The birch in Finland is different as well, but that is because it is a national tree, it is holy. 'You have the feeling you are dealing with something very precious'. Our perception affects nature as it affects us. Wood is a language; an oak is an oak is an oak, and it protests, while birch and beech welcome the caress of the saw. But they all have different dialects according to where they grow.

The Tools

The honest marks of tools appeal directly to the senses and communicate the resistance or pliability of the wood. Honesty is one of Nash's words. He has a touch of the 'Truth to material' attitude of the 20s which is in keeping with his interest in Chinese philosophy. The tool is an instrument of change, metamorphosis, whether the intervention is with man-made tools or the elements: earth, water, air, light or fire. Nash uses them all.

Air and Water

When he was a young man Nash read about Edvard Munch who left his paintings outside for the whole winter, inviting the elements to participate in the creative process, hoping, according to Nash, that his art would thereby become a part of the real world. Certain types of dead wood react drastically to changes in temperature. In two sculptures, *Skirted Beech* and *Crack and Warp Column*, from 1985 and 86 respectively, Nash has made use of the reactions of beech and birch to drying. He has cut two tree trunks into thin slices without completely severing the trunks, and left them for 12 days exposed to a warm wind, causing the wood to warp. The result is two alive and very different pillars. Another experiment uses water. In 1978 David Nash put a large oak ball in a stream in Wales. There it remains. Moss grows on it in the summer and in the winter it rolls with the current and is sometimes covered with ice and snow. It exists with the seasons and its own deterioration. In 1982 he repeated the experiment with a hollowed-out trunk, *River Tunnel*, in a river in Kotoku, Japan, and with three geometrical primary forms – ball, cube and pyramid – in the water at Hatasaka.

Fire

Fire is the most difficult and dramatic tool, and changes the wood from vegetable to mineral. The sight of charred wood is no longer a wood experience, but a carbon experience. The black surface is primarily experienced as a form, whereas untreated wood is primarily seen as a material. Several of Nash's most impressive sculptures, eg

Threshold Column, 1980, and *Seven Charred Rings*, 1986, are charred. In the composition *Three Basic Shapes*, he combines black drawings of objects on paper and the charred objects in a magical image: the idea of things and the things themselves. The latter have actually had to be enlarged to visually correspond to the drawings of them. In *Black Dome, Forest of Dean*, charred chestnut stakes form a small mound. They appear as a deep-black form out of doors and the idea was for the stakes to crumble and become a black spot on the floor of the forest. Instead it has become a playground for children. The very act of lighting a fire and burning wood in ovens of wood, stone, snow and ice, has also been a theme for several of Nash's experiments in such different places as Washington, Japan, Holland, Scotland, Ireland and Wales.

Growth

Using wood is accompanied by a moral obligation to plant trees, just as the Chinese who use clay laid down by their grandparents must leave clay in a pit for their grandchildren. The land Nash owns was once a forest. He now plants trees. In 1977 he began his project *Ash Dome*, which is the work most often associated with his name: 22 ash trees planted in a ring. According to an old English custom, hedges are shaped by bending young trees with the aid of incisions and cutting back. Nash has adopted this method and in approximately 15 years the ash trees will enclose a space.

Like the potter who imagines that the clay clings to an invisible form, Nash is expecting the trees to make a dome-shaped space with time. The project has, however, demanded more manipulation than he likes, so in a new project, *Ash Bowl*, he coaxes the trees to grow as he wishes by planting quick-growing bushes on three sides of each tree so that as they seek light, they will grow in the desired direction. Light and shade are his tools. In 1983 Nash moved a circle of weeds from Wales to the lawn at Serpentine Gallery in Kensington Gardens in exchange for a ring of turf from the park. Whether there is more or less is not important as long as the idea of what one aims to do is precise – Nash compares this 'looseness' with the blue brush strokes in a Chagall painting. Since the show at Serpentine Gallery, he has consciously treated the turf from London as it has been used to, that is mowing it with a lawn mower, while the Welsh weeds have fallen in grace and been removed because they polluted. But the experiment was a good one and humorous.

Positive and Negative Form

The narrow boat-shape, curved or straight, has been a cherished motif of Nash's for years. Visiting Tasmania, he found a large eucalyptus

FROM ABOVE: Running Table, *1978 (restored 1986), Grizedale Forest Sculpture Park; Oak ball in stream in Wales, 1978;* Standing Frame, *1987, white oak, approx 6.7m high*

tree with a scar shaped like a boat gliding downwards, 'almost like an incarnation', says Nash. Cutting the shape out, the saw came right through and removing the 'boat', he experienced the hole in the tree not as a boat, but as space. Later he realised that what he had found was actually the traces of a bark canoe which the Aborigines had cut out of the bark of the living tree. At Ile de Vassivière in 1989 he carved the scupture *Descending Vessel*, 12 metres high, in a spruce tree surrounded by spruce; a revelation of lightness rising heavenwards cleaving a tree. The core is opened up and form and contour are strengthened by letting in the light. An excellent example of the difference between the inner form and the outer case it is born of, is the three-legged oak sculpture *Inside/Outside*. In physical terms, the smaller is heavier than the larger part, but in visual terms, it is the larger which is more weighty because the space emphasises the form.

The Instinct of Trees

Nash works with the instinct of trees, or as in a work at Tranekær, with the instinct of animals. In 1980 he made four drawings: *Sheep Spaces* with earth, berries and leaves, merging the organic qualities of the place with his representations of landscape. At Tranekær he has chosen a stand of old oaks as his space. This is where the sheep stay. For years they have rubbed their backs against the tree trunks and polished them smooth at a height of 50 cm. In this covert, Nash has placed different blocks of oak, shaped so that they can be used for shelter, safety and scratching by the animals. At first one doesn't see them,

one sees the sheep, which in turn see the blocks and use them. It is up to us to take notice of his gentle intervention.

Nash takes our commitment to nature very seriously. He's process oriented but never agitating. His work is full of humour and happy associations to the tangible world: *Standing Frame*, *Running Table* and a ladder of willow in Japan entitled *Man Has Got So Far From Nature That He Needs a Very Long Ladder to Get Back into It*. Picasso would have begun by drawing a bull and ending up with an abstraction. Nash, going in the opposite direction, sees the form in the core of the wood and frees it in the shape of a spoon, a table, a dish, a throne or a comet. Like Brancusi's wood sculptures, they are elementary and archetypal.

Nash does not harbour any romantic notions that nature should remain untouched. Nature is best served with human nurturing. David Nash plants because he uses, and his sculptures breathe rhythmically the way the wood in one of Brancusi's columns breathes, or the way plants breathe and the earth breathes: winter, spring, summer. He uses nature – and serves nature. He experiments and his life is one long discourse with wood, where the dialogue is more important than the results. His aim is to have nature and his work merge into one. In this way art borrows from the irrefutable physical reality of nature, becomes even a part of nature and is thereby sancrosanct.

Based on interviews with David Nash

The 'Ash Dome' in April 1989

David Nash 1989

The Ash Dome, *April 1989*, charcoal on paper, 81 x 113cm

'BIRDS'
DAVID REASON

Blean
March 1994

Dear R

I've been meaning to write to you for some time now, but it has proved a fruitless task looking out for that wee patch of time in which to stretch, settle down and devote myself to tapping out for you a few thoughts, observations and wishes. It is in this way that those who are closest to us are asked too often to show forbearance, since, being first in our hearts and thoughts, they tend to get left until last, until we have time to devote to them. A kind of disengagement, I guess, a sort of special attentiveness, can mark out those things and persons that we value: in life, in writing, in art. So on this occasion I have resorted to another ploy. I have to write a brief article for the magazine *Art & Design*, in relation to a conference on art and nature in Denmark last year,[1] and there's no better way to do so than by composing a letter to you! You don't mind a couple of thousand other readers peering over your shoulder as you scan these lines, do you?

Why write to you, especially, about this? Probably because whenever now my mind turns to questions of the relationship of art, environment and politics, I think of your home town Russe. If I were looking for an example of an occasion on which an artistic intervention helped to change a world, then an outstanding contender is the 1988 exhibition in Russe which dramatised the effects of the Romanian pollution which drifted like a techno-miasma across the Danube. Has an exhibition of art ever before helped spur the development of such a potent political force as Ekoglasnost? I doubt it. Thinking about Russe – about the courage it took to mount such a critical show in Bulgaria before 'The Changes' of 1989, about the fate of those involved, about the role of Ekoglasnost in mobilising dissent against the communist regime – I feel as though I am touching a hard, cold rock of actuality after so long spent trying to pluck my way through the candyfloss of much Western liberal eco-artspeak.

Before 89 the seductive fantasy of human omnipotence (just as endemic but so diffuse in the West) was touched every time money changed hands in Bulgaria, for (do you remember?) the largest steelworks in the nation was the icon on the reverse of the note, where we English have pictured the cultural heroes (and one heroine) of our own new found industry, the production of cultural heritage – and by the shopload! The new Bulgarian notes may have banished the old icons representing the mastery of Nature by Man, but other images took their place: it is, after all, *culture* that truly abhors a vacuum. On the reverse of the first new note that paused a moment in my hand I was intrigued to see a new icon – of an old icon! A medieval wheel of life, representing the cycle from birth to death, replete with the Old Harvester himself bringing in the crop of souls at the end of the season: here, then, nothing less than the subjection of Man to Nature. The wheel turns. The wheel turns, and we are on it or under it, and it seems that its turning is forever beyond our will. You would think that we were wise by now to these plots of either-or, wouldn't you? But clearly not.

The toilets at the hotel in which we stayed for the conference – those expected to be used by women – were thoughtfully provided with small plastic bags for the disposal of sanitary towels and tampons. The picture printed on the front was surely symptomatic of a culture. The one word – *Madame* – politely distanced the woman from her own body: menstruation is not *nice*, my dear, and the language of urbane culture curtains Blood from Being. The image was of a foaming, crashing sea wave, as green as environmentalism, as all-absorbing as only the oceanic can be. *Nature* (this image seemed to express) will take all your dirt, without becoming dirty itself, and you will be left clean and pure. How on earth could a conference deliberating on art and *nature* hope to compete with the routine insertion of the figure of *Madame Nature* into every WC? (These bags now have a different design on them, I learned a couple of days ago. I wonder if our talk about the previous ones had some role in this.)

There is something inordinately comforting, apparently, in believing that there is an identifiable domain of *nature* which is unerringly differentiated from a realm of *culture*. What is *culture* here? I'm not clear, the usages are so shifting and shifty. Sometimes *humanly-produced* is intended, sometimes the

Lynne Hull, Raptor Roost with Hawks, *1988, wood and mixed media, 46cm tall*

75

accent is on *artificial*, at other times it indicates the *changeable* (and, in a sideslip towards a Judaeo-Christian inheritance, it then smells of *corruption*), on yet other occasions a species of *perverse domination* might be indicated (together with its accomplice, the *plan*). This is but a sample of the varieties of *culture*. In each case, *nature* stands conversely. And here something interesting emerges: for not only does *nature*, like *culture*, tread the catwalk of discourse in an ensemble of contradictory meanings (signifying both *spontaneous* and *lawful*, for example), but it is also – as is every supermodel – the object of ambivalent feelings, shot with hate and envy. *Nature* can stand in for our sense of the utterly Other, of the antithesis of all that is congenially human: terrible, sublime, unspeakable. In this sense our attitude towards *Nature* smacks of our fascination with horror: we are abject before *Nature*. But *Nature* can also come to embody our sense of the real possibility of a longed-for state beyond care and sorrow, a paradise beyond strife and contention: it is as though we wished to redeem a promissory note of freedom in a reunion with *Nature*. In this sense, *Nature* is almost a code-word for a kind of nostalgia for the future, for hope.

What this boils down to is this: *Nature* is a *cultural* product, both as a concept, and – in all the ways that can matter to us, because *mattering* is a cultural inflection – it also a *cultural* product. (Another way of putting this would be to emphasise that *Nature* is a vessel of, and for, myth and fantasy.) Of course, we may suppose and suppose that there is somewhere a *nature* that is simply for itself, and this cannot be gainsaid. The importance of this idea of *nature* may be stressed by using expressions such as *wild nature*, to distinguish it from the *humanised nature* of the domesticated countryside, for example. Yet I am unhappy about this further *doubling* of *nature* (as though thought were mimicking cell division) – on two (!) counts. First of all, *wild* and *wilderness* are terms that are not exempt from the vicissitudes of history. Their meanings are choreographed by human interests, practices and knowledges, as Oelschlager (*The Idea of Wilderness*) and Nash (*Wilderness and the American Mind*) among others have amply documented. *Wildness* has its own history, as it were. These studies stand alongside others which painstakingly attempt to tease out the ways in which we humans produce not only a landscape but also a sense of 'the natural'. The most recent of these to come my way is J Stephen Lansing's *Priests and Programmers*, dauntingly subtitled 'Technologies of Power in the Engineered Landscapes of Bali'. Don't be put off, however: this is a marvellously clear, subtle and powerful analysis both of the construction of the Balinese rice-dominated landscape and of the generation of the various beliefs which informed and mystified that world.

When I spoke at the Danish conference, I tried to bring home a similar point by talking about the weather. 'Before setting out for Denmark,' I said, or so the notes I brought home prompt me, 'it is prudent to listen to the weather forecast: unless I know what weather to expect, I don't know what to pack. Packing one's suitcase is an exercise which gives concrete expression to anticipation, to expectation, to anxiety, to hope. Weather exists as an intersection of time and place and me. *The weather is as the weather is*: capricious enough to make us tentative in our claims to knowledge and control, regular enough to make it worth the effort of hazarding a guess about the future.'

To amplify these gnomic remarks, I played a recording of the midday national weather forecast from the previous day's radio broadcast. A Bank Holiday loomed, and the forecaster obligingly told the weather in a narrative decked out with references to sporting activities and family outings. That's one way of telling the weather: a good story, a little explanation, an engagement with human interests. 'In England, we want to know about Bank Holiday Monday weather: where shall we take the kids? Will I be able to whip the garden into order?'

I compared this broadcast with another, of the shipping forecast for the same day – a forecast, needless to say, which spoke to another bespoke interest. The familiar litany unrolled: Lundy, Shannon and Dogger were each mentioned in the right place, barometric figures trotted out in good order, *fairs* and *fallings* coupled the listener to the future. The shipping forecast can be heard as a kind of ritualised performance, an enigmatic list, with variations and repetitions. It conforms to the minimalist strategy: strip away everything which is not absolutely necessary to the characterisation of the weather at that place and time. Of course, lists are always on the verge of the poetic, as the surrealists well knew, since they suppress the conditions, the motivations, the interests that underlie their production. The rationale, the *raison d'être* of the list is always tacit and not articulated within the listing itself. For this reason, the list seduces us into believing that there is something more than what is given to us. The list provokes a fantasy of a power that lies elsewhere, unspoken: and the secret things – the things kept from us, the things people whisper as we leave the room – these are the things which we take to be *true*. The shipping forecast transcends banal narrative: it is an intimation of the mundane sublime.

76

By this device I had hoped to exemplify the processes of cultural construction (the double sense is intended) in a domain of *nature* which most artists have overlooked. (Richard Long is an exception, as also are the otherwise utterly different British Goldsworthy and Japanese Okubo.) Moreover, I wanted to motivate some arguments about the tactics of art making, especially in relation to the advocates of artists' participation in a programme for the re-enchantment of *nature*. This view often sees the successful work of art as one which celebrates both the mystery and the unity (or harmony) of the *natural world*. As you know well, I am convinced that mystery and myth have contributed greatly to the despoliation of the world and its peoples, and that there is more than enough wonder in things as they are, rather than as they appear when drenched by our unbounded desires. Too often, the regressive neoromantic idealisation of *nature* cloaks a corrosive and virulent attitude towards people and produces artworks so anodyne and legible, so shitless, that they qualify as quintessential *eco-kitsch*. (Incidentally, of all that I said on Langeland, it was this trope of weather which stuck in people's minds, it seems. I hadn't expected that the BBC shipping forecast would be such a resonantly cherished item for a Danish audience, but it was, and many participants spoke warmly of listening as a child, with evening drawing on. My observation was even broadcast on radio in Finland, and provoked the first fan mail for several years!)

I'll now return to the thought that prompted this diversion. My second reservation when presented with the view that *wild nature exists for itself* is that the idea of a *nature* 'for itself' actually redeploys the human centredness of the ideas of *nature* from which it is trying to flee. Recently, on an announcement card for a show in New York, Hamish Fulton (an artist whose work I revere) insisted that *wild nature exists for itself*. Well, if the choice is between existing *for itself* and existing *for us* (as raw material, as National Park, as Site of Special Scientific Interest) then I must agree, for it is of the utmost importance that we recognise not only that *nature* has interests (so to speak) that are independent of ours – independent of human existence – but also that our own possibilities of existence are dependent upon *nature*'s own interests being satisfied. In this way of thinking, clearly we depend on *nature* in ways in which *nature* does not depend on us. But to think of *nature's interests* at all is to adopt a fashion of speech, merely: *nature* has no conscious interest, nor any end in view, and so cannot be *for* itself any more than it can be *for* others. The best we can say is: *wild nature exists*. Isn't that enough?

Well, up to a point. Fulton's way of putting the matter establishes the moral dimension of his – and mine, and I hope your – concern with issues of *nature*, *wilderness*, and the (seemingly) non-human directly and economically. My quibbles threaten to dissolve that moral dimension. However, out of naked self-interest, we cannot afford to lose sight of the moral discourse in which these problems are embedded, for, if we do, then it is not some distant horizon of *nature* that is at stake, but our own lives, too. In writing this, I am not thinking primarily of the invisible mycelium of ecological connectedness that sustains our lives and deaths, important as that is, but of the need to recognise that we human beings are ourselves a species of *humanised nature*. If we trash the wilderness out there, then be sure that we are trashing the wilderness within – imagination and desire, dark and light. The domination of *nature* is also and inevitably the domination of *humanised nature*. Tidying up the wild and unkempt places goes with tidying desks, tidying streets, tidying minds.

I'm tempted here to say a word about Lynne Hull's sculpture, although her aspiration and her work are in no way simply illustrative of what I have been arguing. Far from it: her work is its own argument. Although unquestionably relevant to the themes raised in this letter, Hull's sculpture bears on another issue that emerges alongside a wish to displace the human point of view from our dealings with *nature* that is, to whom is environmentally-conscious art to be *addressed*? Much environmentally-sensitive, ecologically-sound art codes its concerns in a symbolic fashion, demanding that the spectator interpret its foregrounded substance, form or process. Hull appears to want her work above all to *make amends*, to count as an attempt to remedy some of the impact of human activity by making interventions in the landscape which are definitely useful to definite creatures. In a landscape where vulture roosting places have been destroyed by overbearing human industry, she installed tall sculptures fit for the fussiest vulture to perch on. However much these objects are worked to be aesthetically telling, the criterion of success is whether or not the sculpture is hospitable to vultures. Hull's is artwork strictly for these birds (or the pine martens   ), and the pleasure we have in them is secondary to – it may even be a consequence of – their fitness to their purpose. There is a long line of European thought which considers artworks to be a kind of *second nature* in their purposed purposelessness. Sculpture for the vulture culture feints towards purposelessness by reorienting its chief usefulness towards interests other than human. In so doing, it invites being considered alongside other examples of *the beautiful in nature*.

I suppose that the upshot of this discussion is that we must not forget how sheerly *difficult* it is to be clear about all this business of *nature* and by extension *environment*. These are not innocent terms, but freight all manner of prejudice and desire. Nature – as is weather – is a cultural category, not a thing but a conception or representation, it is a moment in the way we make sense of our being in the world. And as Brian Wallis argues in his introduction to the collection he edited, *Art after Modernism: Rethinking Representation*: 'Considered in social terms, representation stands for the interests of power. Consciously or unconsciously, all institutionalised forms of representation certify corresponding institutions of power.'

At this moment I will reconnect with what has developed to be a 'red thread' in this writing, that is, the close relationship between the framing of an attitude towards human beings and a simplifying idealisation of *nature* which perpetuates a myth of invulnerable certainty (about, precisely, what is most contentious: the constitution of a *natural* order), of benign harmony, of ineradicable Otherness. The relatedness finds one expression in the turn towards 'primitive' arts and peoples as a touchstone of authenticity, intensity and wisdom. Commonly, the peoples that figure here – Australian Aborigines, North American Indians ('First Nation' peoples), Inuit, !Kung/San, Yanomami: the list is finite but long – are represented in isolation from our world of biros, mortgages and all manner of megabusinesses. Here, Sega and Nintendo have a bigger turnover than General Motors. There, people are quarantined from history. When they make art, it is required to be art made from outside the stringencies of the artworld. They are unable to distinguish the facts of living from the values of the sacred and divine (it is claimed), art and ritual are one, they have incompletely separated from Mother *Nature*. In a compelling contribution to the *Art Journal* for the summer of 1990, Janet Catherine Berlo is clear that this attitude demeans such peoples:

> Arts by the dispossessed have been marginalised in multiple ways. They are outside the main discourses of power (the Euro-centric art world), and even within ethnographic art history they are marginalised once again for failing to be 'authentic', 'pure', 'indigenous' representations. They are not sacred works made of native materials . . . These artists affirm what we too often forget: they are not merely passive recipients of the goods and ideas of the dominant culture. To analyse their art is to recognise that they are active participants in a changing social drama.

The cultural inflection of ab-original peoples is to see them *as nature*: as outside history, as before the corruption of civilisation. This theme has been most tellingly explored recently in Robert Gordon's study of the people of Namibia known variously as the Bushmen, !Kung or San, in his study of *The Bushman Myth*. The idealisation of the !Kung/San as an Edenic people living in a state of 'primitive affluence' overlooked the violent oppression which marked the lives of these peoples generally: the unsavoury offended the educated palate, and the academics and mystics – such as Laurens van der Post, Prince Charles's guru – colluded in the intensification of their misery. The Bushmen fight back: partly by playing up to the demands of the powerful – Bushmen can survive by masquerading as Bushmen, much as women can get by in patriarchal culture by masquerading as women – partly by refusing their allotted role by refusing an all-out immersion in it. For the European colonists, the Bushmen were closer to nature than us, there was more of the animal in them: they made excellent trackers in the police force and army.

This reminds me of Lassie, the Hollywood-celebrated truth-sayer who lived on the brink of shamanic status, able to slip between the animal nature and human duplicity and guile, and of the extraordinary success of *The Track to Bralgu*, not so much a hoax – in similar terms, Castenada's *Don Juan* was no hoax either – as a figure of our desire. Edward Said, examining and cross-examining the Occidental fascination with *Orientalism*, has trenchant things to say on the viciousness of such metropolitan dreaming for those who find themselves invested with the potency of another's Otherness. In *The Forbidden Experiment*, his record of the attempt to bring Victor, the famous feral child of Aveyron, to speech, Roger Shattuck discusses our fascination with 'Wolf Boys' in terms of our desire to hear what it is like to be an animal. Give the pre-civilised child articulate speech and we are agog for his report on the wild side. I suggest that this is part and parcel of the chronic tragedy (if such it be) that Barthes muses on in his discussion of Cy Twombly: that my body is not your body – there is an irreducible and irredeemable gulf between us. We dream of that other whose consciousness is, as Bataille says is the animal's, 'like water in water'. It is a species of nostalgia for that narcissistic bliss of early infancy, in which we were saturated with a maternal world, inseparate.

Here, then, are some terms of debate. Nature: woman: primitive: aboriginal. A familiar series. Nature as benign, as malevolent. As beautiful, as simply whatever it is. As pristine, as improved by human working. As lawful, as spontaneous and irrational. As a larder – of food, of genetic diversity –, as transcending human interests. Human centred, other centred, non-centred. And so on and on and on.

In this connection, I am reminded of two moments which gave me special pause for thought at the conference on Langeland marking the inauguration of the sculpture park at Tranekær. The conference devoted itself by and large to the perennial topics that we touch on when considering the interconnections of art and nature and environment, and the speakers and audience warmed to their – no, our, since I was privileged to be there too – themes, wrapping up snug in a shared sense of impending or actual environmental despoliation and in a conviction that art can re-sacralise a disenchanted world. One Danish speaker counterpointed his inventory of ecological destruction and his anticipations of imminent catastrophe with references to Langeland as it used to be, 100 years or more ago. The people ate what they grew, and so ate in season. They made what tools they needed from whatever resources were to hand. They were well satisfied with, and by, their place. So went his story. His words touched on the image of a small but self-sufficient community; independent, resilient and *balanced*, to use a word which can trade on the implicit sense of a relationship between harmony and sanity. Langeland was presented as an idyllic island effectively isolated from the rest of the world, even from its neighbours. However, later that day, in the afternoon, the conference participants congregated in Tranekær park for the official opening. Imagine my surprise and pleasure to find myself underneath a large Turkish oak, clearly some 250 years old! This fine tree was one of many specimens bought to Langeland from all over the world. The island was no island at all, so far as trade and the spoils of travel were concerned.

Art relating to the landscape must face leading questions. Key amongst these are those that seek to determine the extent to which the work has confronted issues of *prejudice*, of *projection*, and of *provenance*. A work that sits easy in the mind, that delights us with no trouble, is probably preaching to the converted – in other words, it is at home amid our shared prejudices. Only when we are challenged by art are we helped to articulate, scrutinise and unpick what we thought we could take for granted. A lot of work which claims a concern with *nature* is so winsomely communicable that it tells us more about the artworld than about its putative subject matter. Again, an artwork may represent or urge a view of *nature* as benign or malevolent, as sentimental or grotesque – that is, as constituted in response to our own, perhaps scarcely acknowledged, feelings, which become projected into the realm of *the natural* for safety's sake. Sentimental projection tells much more about the artist than about the putative subject matter. (Failure to avoid projection and prejudice result in the denial of the particularity of the natural world – and in becoming something not only *for* but *of* us we assimilate or otherwise deny difference. The world becomes simplified.) Finally, every space is a place – for someone, for something. To act otherwise is at best to act disrespectfully, but it may be to act viciously. As those who work the land know, every field has a name. We can ask: is this work in and of its place?

All this week I have been reading Ohtake's book *Creative Sources for the Music of Toru Takemitsu*, and have learned much. Ohtake discusses Takemitsu's desire to make a music which is part of the 'stream of sounds', a music which accepts – for the listener – whatever happens. A Mozart quartet strives for self-sufficiency, and so the sparrow that testily chatters while I try to listen to it is heard as an intruder. Not so with a piece by Takemitsu, say, *A Flock Descends into the Pentagonal Garden*. The sparrow is welcome to join the flock. I wonder how hospitable, how welcoming, should be an art touching nature?

Takemitsu was inspired at one time by these lines written by the 11 year old Australian Susan Morrison: *'Hours are leaves of life / And I am their gardener / Each hour falls down slow'*.
I used to think that there are two extremes of art, one that induces the suspension of time, and one that encourages time to congeal (which Fellini noticed as he watched Balthus paint). I'm no longer so sure. In all my uncertainty, about this as about so much else, I too find these lines curiously haunting. But to know where that reverie will lead, you must wait for another letter, I'm afraid. I'll find that space soon, I promise. I will make time for you.

With warmest wishes
Dave

Note
1 The Conference (August 28 – September 1993) was held to inaugurate the TICKON project, Langeland, Denmark.

80

THIS ROCK, THIS STREET, THIS EARTH

MARK BOYLE

My ultimate object is to include everything. In the end the only medium in which it will be possible to say everything will be reality. I mean that each thing, each view, each smell, each experience is material I want to work with. Even the phoney is real. I approve completely of the girl in Lyons who insists that it's real artificial cream. There are patterns that form continuously and dissolve; and these are not just patterns of line, colour, texture, but patterns of experience, pain, laughter, deliberate or haphazard associations of objects, words, silences, on infinite levels over many years; so that a smell can relate to a sound in the street, to an atmosphere noticed in a room many years ago. I believe that the electric stimulus given to the brain by these interlocking patterns of reality is the same impulse – though for me by comparison it is luminous and strong – as the aesthetic pleasures generated by brilliant beautiful works in other media. I feel I must feed the concentration; that is necessary to 'dig' reality, to uncover its infinite layers and variations, to juxtapose, to superimpose, to use random techniques, to use emotions, even those that are critically unacceptable such as nostalgia, to use them knowingly and unknowingly, also to refrain from using them, to accept, to be open, to classify and evaluate pain, to make a fool of myself, to laugh, to weep, to glory in the strength of the strong, to appreciate the weakness of the weak, to love my enemies.
ICA Bulletin, June 1965

We'd be on the tube going to work, and Joan would suddenly burst into tears, not just a bit of a snuffle, she would moan, tears would pour down her face and her body would shake with vast sobs of grief. The whole train would be looking at me, as the obvious cause of this terrible pain. I would observe myself playing the concerned, bourgeois husband and I would genuinely be disturbed and horrified at the situation. But I couldn't help noticing at the same time that Picasso had got it exactly right in his *Crying Woman* painting. Except that Joan wasn't green and yellow. By now her face would be a mass of red and maroon and wetness, with bedraggled hair and hands and tears and teeth. And I also noticed that each tear seemed to act like a lens, slightly enlarging and also somehow concentrating light on the skin immediately underneath it, as it made its way down to her chin. When I put my arm around her

shoulders she would say, 'Don't try to comfort me, because you can't!' And she'd gesture towards the *Evening Standard* and there would be a story about a father rescuing one child from a fire but being unable to get back to rescue his wife and the rest of the family. Or there'd be a photograph of a starving child in Africa. Or a story about civil rights' workers being thrown alive into the wet concrete of a dam in some backward southern state of the US. And I would keep my arm round her shoulders and would stare back at the other passengers trying to say with a look, 'It's not hormonal, it's not some kind of misplaced emotion syndrome. It's just that she's right! And all the rest of us have read that story. So how come she's the only one to react like a human being?' We had to stop buying the *Evening Standard* for a while.

One of my very best friends in the whole world found one night that his wife had brought a sick duck into the house. Then there were dogs and cats and a rabbit with a broken leg. Then she brought back homeless people and down and outs and alcoholics. She couldn't bear to think of them out there in the night. And my friend loved her because he had always loved her and because she was so good. But eventually another lady came along with different sensibilities, and he found that he was able to live without the complexities of having to adjust to strangers in his house each evening.

And another time we were trying to tape record snippets of everyday chatter and repartee in Oxford Street without a special microphone. When we got the tape back home we couldn't hear anything except the traffic and the polyglottal roar. Yet when we were there we could hear everything that was said clearly. We had simply filtered out the noise of the traffic and the crowds. Most of us have filters that allow us to suppress the noise we don't want to hear. People whose filters don't work find the noise unbearable.

We believe that we all filter carefully the perceptions of our senses: that we stare at our environment through veils of varying density. Of course, this is necessary. If we walked through the city seeing this urban environment in all its glory, we would become helpless with awe at its brilliance and fascination. We are not preaching. We have never tried to preach to anyone. I think we can all quietly agree that the day of the sermon is over. We are not even recommending a course of action. We wanted to teach ourselves to see. We wanted to see truthfully.

The Boyle Family, Study from the White Cliff Series, 1988, painted fibreglass, 335.2 x 182.8cm; photo James Ryan

We wanted to bear witness to reality. Of course we can only perceive that reality through our senses. Absolute truth would be a perfect description of all reality. The best description of all or part of that reality that our senses and the unconditioned, unprejudiced mind can achieve is what we call truth. The trouble is that here in Hillside House, Crooms Hill, Greenwich beneath the black and yellow clouds that are now beginning to jostle and barge their way across southeast London, there are no unprejudiced and unconditioned minds. Nevertheless in Boyle Family we are constantly and hopelessly trying to work towards this truth. Trying to remove the prejudices that the conditioning of our upbringing and culture impose. Trying to make the best visual description our senses and our minds can achieve of a random sample of the reality that surrounds us. Boyle Family are not social or anti-social, radical or anti-radical, political or apolitical. We feel ourselves to be remote from all these considerations. We want to see if it's possible for an individual to free himself from his conditioning and prejudice. To see if it's possible for us to look at the world, or a small part of it, without being reminded consciously or unconsciously of myths and legend, art out of the past – or present art and myths of other cultures. We also want to be able to look at anything without discovering in it our mother's womb, our lovers' thighs, the possibility of a handsome profit or even the makings of an effective work of art. We don't want to find in it memories of places where we suffered joy and anguish or tenderness or laughter. We want to see without motive and without reminiscence this cliff, this street, this roof, this field, this rock, this earth.

I often feel that we can be extremely limited in our emotional responses. We laugh when we are provided with an obvious punch line or prompted by artificial laughter in a situation comedy. We enthuse when the stars hit a pose that says 'applause' and then the enthusiasm is so often out of all proportion. It's safe to get angry back home with the wife, or when it's sanctioned by PMT, or in the safety and isolation of our own car when you can froth or scream. And you can only weep . . . well, when can you weep in public? If we weep at the movies we invariably come out saying, 'I don't believe I could weep watching crap like that'.

I don't distinguish between natural and man-made. It is part of the arrogance of human beings to set ourselves apart from the rest of nature. I believe that a fork-lift truck, a tower block or a stock exchange are every bit as natural as a cobweb, a bird's nest or one of the big red ant heaps that we saw all over the Central Australian Desert.

What I mean is that we can be walking across a piece of urban wasteland and there's a huge puddle with bricks and half-bricks and worn out wellies submerged in it. And we can see it as a limitless silver sea with entrancing scattered islets, or we can choose not to use our imagination but to try to see it, without filters, as an amazing ordinary glittering puddle littered with bricks and half-bricks and lumps of concrete. If we pick one of the bricks up, and if it's the average mature Glasgow demolition site, we will discover that the brick has a flora and fauna all of its own. We can choose to shake the swarming slaters/wood-lice off it, or drop the brick in disgust, or we can look at them as the wonderful creatures they are. And then there's my hand that's holding the brick or writing these words. A perfectly ordinary, amazing hand. A bit gnarled and twisted by now, but if you even start to think what it is and what it does and how it came to be, or a foot, or an eye or an exquisite average throat. And how an ordinary bloke in a pub, who has a throat, two eyes, two hands, two feet, for a lifetime. How can anyone in possession of all that ever be boring? Only if we have filters of conditioning and snobbery inhibiting us from seeing him clearly. Of course it would be impossible for the human race to survive if everyone went about in a trance-like state of anguish or amazement at this environment all the time. But we decided that we would try to raise the veil, for ourselves, a little bit, some of the time.

When I was quite young I went for a long walk one day with Herbert Read, poet and art critic. Throughout the walk neither of us spoke, until near the end, when I asked what 'inscape' was. He said, 'it was a word invented by Gerald Manley Hopkins to describe a state that no one since has ever fully understood.' We never spoke again, but I have gradually come to some kind of understanding of Hopkins' 'inscape'. It is the inner essential nature of anything. It is *any thing* perceived, or experienced, or felt, without the filters of conditioning. I think young children see the world like this. I think artists must do at least some of the time. I think people who are in love see like this as long as they treasure one another. It is so sad when this most unique and wondrous state is presented as a series of smutty cliches. But then we have to look in wonderment at a system in our world that requires that we look at this most sublime condition as something ugly and disgusting. But this too is part of our amazing environment. And this word, environment, which used to mean the things and forces that surround us, has, I am glad to say, gradually come to mean something completely global. So that everything we can think of is part of our environment. We ourselves, our art, our innermost thoughts and essential nature are all part of the environment. The environment is the inscape of everything.

I remember, after a lecture I gave at the American museum, someone said, 'you keep talking about truth and in the same breath you mention your friend Francis Bacon. Well I've been right around the world and I don't see people screaming everywhere.'

I said, 'Sometimes if we're going to be aware that people all around us are screaming we're going to have to be prepared to open our eyes and our ears and our minds and we're going to have to be prepared to weep.'

The Boyle Family, FROM ABOVE: Study for the Westminster Series with Kerb and Pavement Light, 1988, painted fibreglass, 122 x 122cm, photo James Ryan; Street Study from the Westminster Series with Yellow and Red Lines and Pub Cellar Trapdoor, 1989, painted fibreglass

IAN HAMILTON FINLAY

CLASSICISM, PIETY AND NATURE
AN INTERVIEW BY PAUL CROWTHER

Ian Hamilton Finlay's work consists of texts and objects incorporating poems, quotations, aphorisms, slogans and word plays, drawn from or alluding to extremely diverse literary, historical, and philosophical contexts. The texts or text/objects are not printed or made by him personally, rather they are executed by craftspersons on the basis of Finlay's detailed specifications. This creative process also informs his important garden works. These involve not only the organisation of landscapes according to Finlay's designs but the siting of object-texts as an integral element within that organisation. The most developed space of this kind is Finlay's own domicile – Little Sparta, at Dunsyre in Scotland.

At the heart of all Finlay's work is a unifying theme – the continuing relevance of the classical tradition. In all art there is a dialectic of nature and culture, but in classicism this finds its most diverse and extreme embodiments. The classical tradition centres on discourses of purification and clarification which seek to elevate the human being above the merely natural. This elevation can involve the idealisation of form, but equally well, it can involve a more catalytic process wherein a strategic juxtaposition of nature and artefact serves to activate the spiritual significance of the former. Finlay's oeuvre can be located along the entire continuum between these two poles.

But why should classicism understood in these terms be of continuing significance? One superficial answer is to see it as a form of conservative critique, a yearning for 'back to basics' and a cosy time when values were regarded as absolute and eternal. Now whilst there are strands of this facile yearning for illusions of illusion in contemporary culture, they do not characterise Finlay's work. His output is altogether more *dangerous*, in the best sense.

To understand this one must consider Finlay's major existential preoccupation, namely culture's loss of piety and total secularisation. What is at issue here, is not a loss of religious faith, but the decline of our ability to think in terms which can *honour and express* those ultimate questions and situations which make discourse of any sort, possible. This loss of piety embraces both the content and form of contemporary life. Relationships between people more and more conform to stereotypes, and public discourse more and more

takes the form of mere chatter. The pressure to conform is absolute – sustained on one side by the banal 'back to basics' authoritarianism of right-wing governments, and on the other, an insidious left-McCarthyist culture of 'political correctness'. In such a context, questions of truth are elided. What counts, rather is existential success measured in terms of exciting controversy (by mere allegation or whatever means) for its own sake, or mere sensationalism as such. This also extends to the realm of art. Damien Hirst, for example, devises some formally interesting works which are meant to evoke fundamental thoughts about nature, personal relationships, and mortality. These links are certainly made, but in a gimmicky rather than searching way. Their real target is the sensibility of the tabloids – to shock at the same level. And in this they succeed. The boundaries of art, however, are not affected one iota. For after Duchamp, Berlin Dada, and 60s performance art, we already know that, in principle, *anything goes* – or to recast this in a 1990s idiom 'Everything must go'.

The 'Everything' which 'must go', is reality in its depth of being. In contemporary culture, the distinctions between reality and mere simulacra, and between authentic existence and mere therapy (discovering who you really are' etc) are collapsed. There are those – such as Baudrillard who imagine that this collapse is a total one. It is not. For the human sensibility is not simply a wax tablet upon which the banal ephemera of contemporary history impresses itself. It has the capacity to mediate the present and its trivia, in more critical and metaphysical terms.

This is where Finlay's art proves decisive. In its most extreme manifestations, the classical tradition seeks to purify and perfect the real, by clarifying its essential structures. This aesthetic enterprise is, however, more than an aesthetic. For an aesthetic of this sort involves not just a struggle between the immutable and the mortal at a contemplative level; it entails, as well, an ethics and a politics. The French Revolution with its dialectic of reason and terror is the perfect example of this. Finlay's texts, objects, and gardens explore all aspects of this, in both explicit and implicit terms. The explicit dimension focuses on his use of overt French Revolutionary iconography – juxtaposed with classical precedents, and contexts which affirm its contempo-

Nuclear Sail *by the lochan, photo David Paterson*

FROM ABOVE: In the Wild Garden, Little Sparta; A corner of the Wild Garden, Little Sparta; On the way to the Upper Pool, fragments of a supposedly entire but buried Corinthian Column, photos Peter Davenport

rary relevance. The implicit dimension concerns his linkage of all these elements to nature and the implements of warfare in more general terms. The means by which these evocations are achieved – whether in texts, text-objects, or gardens – are *concrete*. That is to say, rather than operate at the level of theory alone, they present a fusion of idea and reality, wherein the two elements are inseparable. They manifest aesthetic ideas. In Finlay's work, therefore, private and public concerns are embodied in a form which allows *consideration*.

It is important to stress this point. For to offer for consideration means that the creator is not simply telling the recipient what to think; yet neither is the recipient placed in an illusory position of absolute neutrality. One is free to choose from the possibilities opened up by the artist.

All these considerations are vital in relation to Finlay's treatment of landscape. There is one current approach to this topic which sees human intervention as something which must go. Let nature speak for itself; let it work on broadly its own principles; let's be ecological. Now, of course, the natural world has suffered terrible depredations through industrial and commercial exploitation. But Ecology as a doctrine can be just as bad in its intellectual ramifications, in so far as it aspires to be a *world-view*. To see nature as a benign self-supporting system with which we need to be in 'rhythm', is to see it in fundamentally anthropocentric terms (for 'eco-system' read 'economy'). But how nature is, *in itself*, is something no human being could ever know. We always view it through culture, and this means in terms of different historical and social perspectives. There is no 'return' to nature *per se*; only positive and negative interpretations of it. To be 'true' to nature means to engage with it in terms of this diversity. One must give it *consideration* and acknowledge its Protean structures rather than make it conform to some pseudo-authentic stereotype.

Finlay's treatment of nature is one which does such justice to it. For in his work, nature never exists raw. It is acknowledged as the site of human endeavour and self-understanding, but without ever being treated as a mere resource. With Finlay, nature and humanity inhabit one another in many different guises. One of the most disturbing of these is in the culture and artifice of Nazism. Here, a vocabulary of classical forms, and rational planning *vis-à-vis* the state and implements of warfare, are used to justify a *natural* order of things. This, of course, is founded on an ideology of innate biological differences between races, wherein one group is seen as intrinsically superior to the others. In this context the drums of culture veritably throb to the rhythms of nature.

The classical tradition gives a continuity to western culture, but it is an ambiguous one, which never excludes its Other ie nature. Finlay's most controversial works, notably *Osso* face this issue, and open out a space for consideration, rather than the over and simplistic *pro* or *con* attitude which the conformist mentality of contemporary culture demands.

And, of course, Finlay has been consistently punished for this. Since the early 1980s he has been persecuted by Strathclyde Regional Council for his attempts to establish his domicile – Little Sparta – as something more than an out of the way tourist resource. Matters came to a head in this respect in early 1983, when the Sheriff's officers attempt to force a warrant sale on Little Sparta were thwarted by the 'Saint-Just Vigilantes' – a group of Finlay's supporters. Perhaps even more disturbing are the circumstances surrounding the French government's commission for a garden to celebrate the Bicentenary of the Revolution. The commission was withdrawn due to a dubious campaign of slander and allegation, based on bizarre misrepresentations of the planned work.

Finlay continues to maintain a prodigious and diverse output of work, despite and, perhaps, because of, the age's unwillingness to countenance anything but the superficial, the simplistic, and conformist. The following interview is based on conversations with Finlay which took place in February 1994.

Paul Crowther *How far do you think that the early jobs you had, working as a shepherd, working out of doors, disposed you towards an interest in perhaps one day creating a landscape of your own?*

Ian Hamilton Finlay I have created a landscape of my own because the ground was here around the house. I mean I might have made something quite different, I might have made films or whatever. My particular talent is for making use of whatever possibility is there. Of course my father's family come from Hopeton. My uncle was a night-watchman there and my grandfather was head of the sawmill. I was quite a country boy.

– Did you have any experience of gardens before you moved to Little Sparta?
No.

– So this was the first one.
As I say, the gardens were proposed to me by the ground being there rather than me proposing it. I can easily imagine that if I had been in some other circumstances, I would never have had a garden and would have done something quite different.

What was your original idea? How far did you conceive Little Sparta developing or did you just

play on the basis of ideas as they came along?
Yes, the question is really for somebody other than me because my life has always been so desperate one way or another. At that time complete lack of money was the problem. The garden's now an achieved fact, quite famous internationally but I don't think people realise what a struggle it was to begin with. In fact all I had was a spade for a long time! There wasn't any money to buy plants, but in those days one was still able to dig up plants and wild flowers. After a time I became quite inspired, not so much from inside but from outside. A cloud or something descended on me and I became absolutely obsessed with the vision of a classical garden, which was absolutely absurd considering this was just a moorland and I only had a spade! However the vision was very real and because of the very disparity between the fact and the dream, it never really worried me about the acres of heather etc. The first works I added were quite like Magritte's incongruous classical artefacts on a hillside and people said 'but you can't do this sort of thing here'. These comments didn't really worry me. To begin with the garden was greatly attacked in Scotland, and even when the first book on it was produced in America called *Selected Poems*, it was reviewed on the BBC, and the reviewer was very unpleasant about the garden. It would be quite interesting to hear this review now.

– How far do you find that the garden provides inspiration for other objects which will be exhibited independently of any garden concepts?
Well once I'd got on my way with the garden I began to see the possibilities of it. Thereafter I became interested in doing things away from here and then by chance a German architect from Stuttgart, who knew my concrete poetry on the page but didn't know I could garden, came to Scotland for a holiday and said would I like to design a garden for the Max Planck Institute in Stuttgart. So I did a little set of works for that.

– When was that?
Oh heaven knows, nearly 20 years ago. Then perhaps as a result of that the Director of the Kröller Müller Museum in Holland commissioned me to do something there and of course that was seen by a lot of people. I really became very fascinated probably more than with things I had got to do away from here but of course I still like doing the garden here. I'm just a wee bit disconcerted that people regard it as my major work. I've got a lot of things going on which people don't know anything about. This year another book will be done on them separately.

– Do you find it something of a paradox that your relationship to Little Sparta is determined by the fact that you live here and yet you are now designing gardens that you have never seen physically and probably never will see?
Yes, but people create a great mystique about this, I don't really find it a problem. I mean I have an associate and she will go and look at a place and take photographs and we will get plans and you can get a very clear idea of what the place is like. I don't move existing works into another garden. The place must propose the works to me.

– Could you explain how the name 'Little Sparta' appertains to classical culture?
It was a quite deliberate ideological gesture. You know that Edinburgh is called the Athens of the North and I wanted to make it clear that I had a quite different ideology. I think 'Sparta' has certain reverberations which are pleasing to me and of course Sparta has a very influential role in the French Revolution which is important to me. Actually, Stonypath is the name of the cottage and I think of the surrounding territory as Little Sparta. I managed to get that name on to the map. Every ten years or so the Ordinance Survey people come and ask you about place names, and that's how it got on.

– This appears to be a convenient point to ask a specific question and then a more general one. The specific question concerns your controversy with Strathclyde Regional Council.
It's not a controversy – it's a war!

– You put the view forward that your work at Little Sparta is a temple?
No. The Garden Temple is a *specific* building. After the garden had been here for between 10 and 15 years I became aware of a fundamental problem. It concerns piety and the total secularisation of culture. I wanted to actualise the conflict between my own vision and that of the surrounding culture and at this point I had already made the old building into a gallery which was officially listed as a gallery. And then I decided that the word gallery now does not mean what it used to mean, say in Victorian times. The gallery is now merely an aspect of tourism and this is a false description of what is here. So I changed the building into a garden temple and whereas before the building had existed to house works, now the works – permanently sited in the building – existed to define the building as a temple. It is a sort of inversion of the original situation. And when I set out to get the evaluation rule changed, they at first refused to change it from gallery to garden temple, they said that 'garden temple' wasn't in the computer etc! I said 'this is ridiculous because the term occurs in every reputable garden history and I live not only in Strathclyde Region but in Britain and Western Europe, and I have every right, as a citizen to stand in that

FROM ABOVE: In the Wild Garden, Little Sparta, a variation on a theme by the German artist Johann Christian Reinhardt, photo Antonia Reeve; A set of large stones inscribed with a sentence from Saint Just: 'The Present Order Is The Disorder Of The Future'; A corner of the lochan, the column bears an inscription from Saint-Just: 'The World Has Been Empty Since The Romans', photos Peter Davenport

perspective and organise my life in that perspective'. After many years, I managed to get this description changed. Then I pointed out that I thought that the building should be exempt from rating because any building that is used according to law wholly or mainly for religious purposes and belongs not to an individual but to a body is so exempt. I would say that the body is either the classical tradition as such because I regard my work as not being unique to myself but being part of a tradition, or to the Saint-Just Vigilantes, a fluctuating body of people who have acted on behalf of little Sparta. The problem was that though the name had been changed, as far as Strathclyde Region was concerned, the content was still the same. I've always called it a war because I felt that I wasn't asking for special privileges for artists but just asking that the law be taken into account. Unfortunately the Region has behaved consistently as if they owned the law, not as if it was theirs and mine and everybody's. When the law is ignored, you are in a state of war. And of course there was the famous day of battle when the Sheriff's officers came to remove objects, and were repulsed by the Saint-Just Vigilantes. This could never be repeated because from then on the Region had great respect for what the Saint-Just Vigilantes could achieve, and would never walk into such a trap again. But now they are taking me to court and I suppose the outcome might be that I lose the case. It is really a question of levels, and if this other level that I am talking about is allowed to be part of reality, then I would win the case. But I fear that in a completely secularised culture, this other level won't be allowed to be part of reality and this is precisely my battle. I would insist that this other level is part of reality and nothing to do with the whimsy of the individual. But I suppose that I'll loose the case because this level won't be allowed into it and then I suppose I will have to choose between my principles and going to prison. We'll see.

– *It is quite interesting that even something which appears nominally to be just a dispute between you and a council has broader ramifications.*
Yes, the dispute is of no interest in itself. Its interest is precisely because it actualises what I see as one of the crises of the age. And I feel very disappointed that although the ordinary press has written about it, the art critics etc have avoided writing about it; or else it is treated as a dispute between an individual and a bureaucracy.

– *So your point is that it is a lot more than that.*
Well obviously, I mean, it is very easy to get support as an individual fighting a bureaucracy, but I am trying to avoid just that – I got a rubber stamp made saying 'Citizens have a right to rigorous bureaucracy'. You must be very careful about who's on your side.

– *Well of course the problem of who's on your side is much involved in the bigger controversy surrounding your garden works and especially the Paris commission.*
I can't see this as a bigger controversy. They're really part of the same controversy and for whatever reason I seem to have a certain talent for, I don't know, actualising these problems.

– *Now the story of the Paris commission, is that the commission was given to you as part of the French Revolutionary . . .*
Bicentenary and it was to make a garden on the site of the original building where the Three Estates met. So that really, if you could say that the revolution began anywhere it would be precisely this point. But the original building has long since vanished and there were just dilapidated sheds and cobblestones and things. I worked out this garden which was to be opened by the President. The proposal was completely accepted and everything was ready to start work when this campaign of disinformation, as the French government later called it, broke in a really big way. It was quite unprecedented. A radio programme at peak time accused me of Nazism and anti-Semitism and said that the garden was going to be filled with swastikas – complete madness! The broadcast was in the morning and the government cancelled the garden in the afternoon. They later wrote a letter saying that the reason for this was that the campaign of disinformation was so great that if they hadn't given in to it, it would have ruined the whole Bicentenary. I suppose that there was a feeling that it was very annoying for France to choose a Scottish person to make the centre piece for the Bicentenary. There was a lot of jealousy. And then of course there was this other thing of the pleasure people take in allegation.

– *This seems to be an idea that is preoccupying you somewhat – the idea of the culture of allegation. Could you say a little more about this?*
It wouldn't preoccupy me if it wasn't done to me and it is not of great interest except in so far as it is only one aspect of this problem of secularisation – and not the most interesting aspect. Since I have to deal with it, however, I have to be concerned about it. When there is a kind of madness in an age, the age usually shows itself incapable of dealing with that madness and it has to be dealt with by the next age and anyone who tries to oppose the madness becomes automatically a lone voice and marginalised and so on. As far as I can see it, I would say that the great paradox is that, so to speak, the arithmetical number of possible allegations against people in terms of political incorrectness has grown and grown. But in all this there is no concept of a good society or of human decency or of any of those

things that would traditionally be the basis of moralising. This is the mystery and the madness which is very difficult to put into words. But it is clear that *this* kind of moralising precedes from a certain destructiveness and hatred, and has nothing to do with love, affection, beauty etc. People who support me often suggest that the allegations are due to misunderstandings of my work. But this was clearly not the case. It's quite clear to me that the people who make the allegations are dependent on inventions. At the centre of the Paris thing was my work *Osso* which on a narrow level would be a specifically anti-Nazi work, but when it was exhibited, it was part of a sequence of works at an exhibition in Arque, Paris. The space in Arque was a very long, continuous curving space which I thought was a very difficult one to fill, so I decided to do a series of works so that each work would be in one sense independent but at the same time related to all the others. The culminating works were very perfect cubes with inscriptions related to neo-Platonism, Plotinus and so on. They were a kind of summit to the project. The first work represented matter as a kind of negativity and this was the work *Osso*. The work was explained and so on but it was used by others as a text to illustrate my supposed Nazism and anti-Semitism. But of course they never described the work correctly. They described it as consisting only of Waffen SS lighting flashes which was not the case because at either end in the third sequence is added the 'o' which gives the Italian word for bone. They never gave the work its title or showed photos of it and then later when it was exhibited at the first exhibition at the Liverpool Tate, everybody could see that the work was not as it had been described. So then my detractors invented the story that there were two *Osso* works, and that the one in the Tate was not the one exhibited in Paris! Complete madness! And in the Tate catalogue there was even a photograph of the work in its Paris context, but even then my detractors claimed that the work was a slab of marble heaped with bones! Complete fantasies. So there was no misunderstanding, just deliberate, destructive invention.

– How far do you see this response to your work as being characteristic of the secularisation of an age? I am just wondering if there is a parallel between that notion and the kind of notion which someone like Heidegger talks about as 'das Man', a concept which signifies the anonymous character of a culture where people act according to stereotypes, where there is no authentic communication between individuals. It seems to me, in other words, that this view you are proposing is very symptomatic of a certain tendency in 20th-century philosophy which sees the rise of an industrial society as profoundly alienating.

Of course when I found parallel utterances in Heidegger and so on, these preceded my own experiences but of course it was very reassuring to find these things formulated. But for a long time, I mean 25 years or more, it has been clear to me that major characteristics of our age have involved the complete absence of piety and all the consequences of that. I find this to be completely unacceptable, I can't possibly feel that I can live in any normal way in a society in which piety is banished. In fact, the situation is more extreme. So really my role has been that of dissident, It seems to me that all Western societies have had their dissidents, including Russian if you can count that as a Western society, but the dissidents take different forms according to the condition of that particular culture. We've now reached a stage where the dissident is the traditionalist. It's just a great muddle, the age has ceased to try and think about its own condition. The age hasn't even invented its own vocabulary; it uses the vocabulary from an earlier age. In fact when the war with the Regional Council started this was demonstrated clearly, as also when I requested the Scottish Arts Council to intervene as a bureaucracy which as part of its duties advises the government at all levels and on all matters concerning the arts. When I asked the SAC to say to the Region that buildings like the garden temple had such and such a content, they refused to do it. The 22 elected members solemnly voted to express no opinion! I thought the Arts Council would be delighted that here is a problem crucial to the age which has its basis in a concrete situation, and I thought they would have called an international conference and embraced the problem fully. But they pushed the problem away, as so did the art critics, and treated it as some kind of joke or the classic thing of lone individual confronting a bureaucracy, an absolute parody of my position which is actually that of a tradition confronting bureaucracy.

– Clearly all the work that you do has a very strong level of philosophical or theoretical content even if we don't mean philosophy in the most narrow sense. I wonder if there is any sense in which you would describe yourself as subscribing to a kind of 'Naturphilosophie'?
On the contrary, the great distinction I make is between nature and culture. I sometimes use the Nazi imagery to represent nature as opposed to culture which I usually represent by the French Revolution or neo-Platonism or whatever. But of course I know that landscaped gardens can be dominated by the idea of nature as the good and this is the most absolute heresy that there can possibly be! One thing that I think is strange is that people do, to a certain extent, see the idea content in my work, but I think that my real achievement, such that it is, is to organise bits of

landscape and things, make good compositions out of grass, trees, flowers and artefacts. But I think the thing that I am really good at is what I call the lyrical. It seems to me that every situation has got its own possibilities and the poet is the person who can most or best see the extent of those possibilities. And for example the battle with the Sheriff's officers was very fascinating because nobody had seen before that the region regarded the warrant sale as like the atom bomb or something. And I saw that because this is a great kind of force we could really do something with it, and I made this kind of battle scenario. But no one could say whether this was a 'happening', an event or an actual battle. What was it? It has not yet really been defined. But I saw that one could by lyrical art make this construction out of this material and everybody who was present was absolutely thrilled with it and enjoyed it very much. And thereafter the warrant sale was never – nobody has ever said this but it is true – the warrant sale was never an effective weapon on the part of the region. People discovered that you could stand up to it and a farmer's wife rang up and said 'I congratulate you, you have raised the whole standard of warrant sales!' It is just that one has to see in actuality its lyrical possibilities. My work is the very opposite of making a division between the real and idea, to me the real is the material which is to embody the idea. This is what excites me. Like this recent exhibition of mine in Munich, where from the museum – the Lenbachhaus – you can actually see the bases or pedestals where Hitler's own temples were. These have always fascinated me because they were originally sort of Nazi shrines and then they were changed by history. Quite recently they had a competition in Munich where they wanted to redesign the whole area and they wanted to replace them with other buildings. And then there was a great dispute. Some people felt that the pedestals should remain as a kind of warning and the Greens wanted them to remain because they had been colonised by wild flowers. It's really amazing that the building begins as a Nazi shrine and it ends as a Green Party shrine. In neither case is it to be touched, it is to be completely sacred. This is the evolution of the history of the idea. So I made two very large models with my proposals of what could be done with the temples. But the proposals arose out of the dialectic between these controversies and viewpoints, which I find fascinating. I suppose this is central to my work, this refusing to accept reality simply as a given. But really the world is what I work in so to speak, and the garden is part of that too.

– One thing you have already touched on a number of times is the fact that you see your work as part of the classical tradition. In the 1980s in painting especially there were some similar attempts to revive neo classicism in a kind of peculiar post modern form. Do you see your gardens and your other objects as an authentic living classicism or are you going to say that what you do is something different from classicism, as it's traditionally understood?
My work can't be a repetition of classicism as it was but it would not interest me at all if it was not authentic. The point is that I *mean* it. You see I don't understand or feel the past as other people seem to feel it. I regard the French Revolution as being not very far away at all. It is very real to me. I can't feel any distance in space between me and the French Revolution any more than when I read Hegel. When I read Hegel, I do not think that this kind of thing belongs to the past, it seems to me to belong now. Similarly when I read Heraclitus, they are all real to me. I live in the same world where the French Revolution took place, where Heraclitus lived and I expect the culture to do the same. But now it is a crime – a crime not to live in the fashionable instant. Many times I have been asked why do you read the Greek pre-Socratics? Of course behind this question is the fact that we know Heidegger read the classics and we know Heidegger is a very suspect figure, how could you justify this? This is all what goes on in all these questions.

– I am quite interested in what you say here because this relates closely to the philosophy that I put forward in my books which is all about there being constants in human experience whereby there is no absolute gap between past and present; there is always a universal core which recurs under different historical conditions.
I don't have such a view as a *theory*, it is just how I actually experience the world. But I notice that other people don't experience it in this way. They regard the French Revolution or Robespierre as some kind of remote monstrous event or person to them, or Heraclitus as someone that you would study, not a philosophy which you would experience in the world. I suppose I am saying to the Strathclyde Region you must allow that the French Revolution is part of the present as well as part of the past. When the law talks about religion, since it doesn't say Christian religion, this can also mean David's *Festival of the Supreme Being* made for Robespierre.

– Do you regard Little Sparta as a single work, a single concept, or do you see it as a kind of site where lots of other works are situated?
I could make a place of that size as a single conception, if someone gave me the money, but without money you can only pursue one corner at a time. And in the beginning I was learning all the time about what you could do. I didn't know anything about plants or stone. I just had to discover it for myself because the sculptors and

people didn't know about it. I'd have thought that the sculptors and letter-carvers would know how you sited stones but they didn't really know much at all. Their interest in the stone ended when it left the workshop. Of course there is a whole tradition, but the tradition has to a certain extent been lost. I mean people often say, my garden is very Japanese but there could be nothing more stupid. I know what they mean, what they mean is that I use art in a serious way using trees, but they are probably quite unaware of the whole tradition.

– Do you think there is still a lot more scope to develop Little Sparta?
Yes, I want to build a sort of temple at the end of the loch, but I don't have any money and there is a dispute about the ownership. Anyway, my present intention is to somehow have this little temple in place by May. I don't know if I'll manage it or not. After that I have this plan to do a pyramid for Saint-Just: there's plenty to do but everything is conditioned by money. I never have any grants.
– So literally your whole career had been built on

selling objects and then getting commissions from whoever you get commissions from.
Yes but it is very difficult to sell works, I am quite well known now but I still don't sell very much. Money has always been a problem, not such a problem as it was, it used to be a problem to find enough to eat and to keep the garden clippers sharp. But since the bank have provided me with an overdraft it is not so bad as it was, but of course when I come to the end of my overdraft then I will have to stop. You have exhibitions but you don't always sell very much and the works are very expensive to do, stone is very expensive. I mean everything is a desperation and my own lack of talent is also a sense of desperation.

– In what sense do you mean lack of talent?
I haven't got very much talent, one just has to harvest this lyrical thing we talked about, but I think I don't really have much talent. If I want to get a line correct it takes miseries and I have to worry about it until I am absolutely worn out.

By the Upper Pool, Little Sparta, photo David Paterson

ACER PSEUDOPLATANUS

MICHAEL PETRY

ACER was a two day siting of works that sought to bring awareness to the plight of the Sydenham Hill Woods in November 1993. The woods are one of the largest surviving fragments of the Old Great North Wood, and are managed by London Wildlife Trust on behalf of Southwark Council. The future maintenance funding of the woods is in doubt, and without this maintenance, the woods would become hazardous and give the authorities grounds for their destruction and make them ripe for private development. The Trust, with much local support, has fought off such threats since 1985, and has created a site that is an important resource for education, recreation and conservation in the centre of South London. The curator, Gloria Carlos selected artists who live in the city and whose work does not usually deal with such issues. Their response grew from the woods and its circumstances, making the context not only a physical, but a psychological one. The artists were invited to visit the woods to select a site. No two artists chose the same site. Their projects were discussed for feasibility and impact on the woods. The artists had only one day to install the works. Sited throughout the landscape, viewers had to traverse the entire woods to see all of the projects. The overriding fear of the loss of the woods was echoed by the limited time of the installation. All the works were intended to be sympathetic to the woods, and as such did not involve the destruction of any trees or create any permanent change or damage.

Phyllida Barlow created *Once Upon a Time* from seven wood, foam and cloth objects and placed them throughout the oldest grove in the woods. They had a natural appearance of pod-like seeds, trellises and dovecots, but at the same time the brightly-coloured objects could have been dropped from a spaceship. They were, and were not of the land. They hinted at a possible outcome for the woods, while essentially referring to themselves as biomorphic and rural objects.

Gloria Carlos erected five white freestanding plaster sculptures that looked as if they were the roots of some mysterious species of plant, or were perhaps some new type of fungus. Their plantlike qualities were offset by the vague possibility that they were termite hills on LSD or toxic waste. The objects sprang from the ground and yet their boastful beauty was at odds, or perhaps highlighted, by their fragility.

John Coleman placed three lifesize *Travellers* each of which 'adopted the markings of his surroundings'. Slightly sinister as they looked down from their vantage points, they had the feel of gameskeepers or woodsmen guarding the woods from poachers. They were viewing as much as they were viewed. They were static but seemed only to be resting, soon to return to their duties or another time.

An Offering by Debbie Duffin placed a small black and white photograph of leaves in a black wooden frame in the window remains of a ruined architectural folly. A view of nature, the artifice of nature, and nature, all seen at the same time from an isolated manmade tableaux. A simple intervention commenting on the complexity of interacting with the natural world.

Mathew Frith constructed a windbreak from fallen leaves out of which a white stag leapt towards the viewer for his *Deer Dear Hart: The Prince is Dead*. The stag was surrounded by a heart made from silver metallic starter motors that he had found discarded in the woods. In Frith's work, romantic, mythic, and near Arthurian notions of the land butt heads with harsh reality.

For *Haute Danse,* Sharon Kivland constructed a ball room setting high up in the tree, using photographs of chandeliers. Each piece was covered by an oval sheet of engraved glass bearing the name of an 18th century French peasant dance that had been co-opted into the Court. Each of the dances featured high-spirited leaps in the air. The natural light was in great contrast to the warm glow depicted in the images. Viewers were forced to strive to read the inscriptions as the elevated placement and reflective quality of the glass so successfully mimicked the leaves and bark.

In Craig Rosborough's *Memoria Artificia* he labelled a circle of trees with small red, white and black (standard issue) enamel London street signs informing the viewer that they were in Leicester Square. From the centre, wherever one looked, the viewer saw the possibility of the encroaching city supplanting nature. While the work itself was jolly, playful and ironic, its presence was rather depressing.

Naomi Siderfin used an old tennis net to catch handmade butterflies, which were also glued to tree trunks with brown molasses. Caught up in unsuspecting yet alluring devices, the butterflies

FROM ABOVE, L TO R:
Phyllida Barlow, Once Upon a Time; *Debbie Duffin,* An Offering; *Gloria Carlos, freestanding plaster sculptures; John Coleman,* Travellers

floundered and looked ready-packaged for a living room wall, tragically encased, as the woods themselves might be, in circumstances beyond their control.

Lucy Smith sited a male and female stone guardian at the entrance of a disused railway bridge that sat deep in the woods. The line was built to service Crystal Palace for the Great Exhibition. The sculptures' smiling faces seemed to be a reassuring presence, their stoic stability in direct contrast to the endangered site.

My contribution, *North-True North: A Question of Scale*, consisted of a 120-foot line of clothing on either the magnetic or true north axis of the woods, powdered with yellow pigment. The pigment was the same colour as the fallen acer leaves and reminiscent of spring pollen. Visually, the seasons were in opposition. The work questioned the concept of science's infallibility in describing the physical world by the act of subjective aesthetic description and in the open deceitfulness of not allowing the viewer to know which axis the line was sited. The largest male gesture was also the most fragile.

The fragility of the exposed woods was unluckily emphasised by the systematic vandalisation of the works at dawn on the last day of the project. It seemed a perfect metaphor for the wholesale destruction of ancient woodlands throughout the UK, where motorways continually carve their way through, or golf course's pave over such important historical nature reserves.

FROM ABOVE: Mathew Frith, Deer Dear Hart: The Prince is Dead; *Sharon Kivland,* Haute Danse; *Craig Rosborough,* Memoria Artificia; *Michael Petry,* North-True North: A Question of Scale